0173   NB

HARDWOOD HEAVEN

Basketball in Kentucky
1895 to 1966

HARDWOOD HEAVEN

Basketball in Kentucky
1895 to 1966

Editor
TOM THURMAN

Introduction by
DAVE KINDRED

Principal Writer
MICHAEL KELSAY

Based on the documentary

BASKETBALL IN KENTUCKY
Great Balls of Fire

from Kentucky Educational Television
and
The Honorable Order of Kentucky Colonels

The publisher wishes to thank the many people who contributed their time, talent and assistance to this publication: Tom Thurman, Mary Ann Carpenter, Craig Cornwell, Donna Moore, Earl Cox, Walter McCord, Nicole and Knox Gunn, Bill Morison, and the Honorable Order of Kentucky Colonels, especially Mike Molloy, Jim Lindsey, and Glen Bastin.

Published in the USA by
Butler Book Publishing Services Inc.
P.O. Box 7311
Louisville, KY 40207

Editorial and Production Director: Bill Butler
Design and page production: Nicole Gunn

ISBN 1-884532-46-2

Printed in Canada by Friesens Printers through Four Colour Imports, Louisville, KY

Text and images in this book are principally derived from the documentary, "Basketball In Kentucky: Great Balls of Fire," underwritten by a grant from The Honorable Order of Kentucky Colonels and produced by Kentucky Educational Television.

The Kentucky
Network

"WHAT IS IT about basketball in Kentucky that endures from one generation to the next? A high school basketball game lasts 32 minutes; a college game lasts 40; players play for a few years and move on; coaches might last a few more; but they all come and go. What lasts is the affection and interest of fans, the ordinary Kentuckians whose hearts rise and fall a hundred times a season in perfect unison with their favorite team's fortunes."

—From *Basketball In Kentucky: Great Balls of Fire*

The Honorable Order of Kentucky Colonels

Among the goals of The Honorable Order of Kentucky Colonels is the preservation of Kentucky history. Of special interest to Colonels is the history of our people. Certainly during the 20th century, basketball became an important part of our lives as individuals, as communities and as a state. The Kentucky Colonels who make up the Honorable Order, a non-profit, charitable organization, are pleased to join with KET in presenting this documentation of the History of Basketball in Kentucky.

The Colonels History

The title Kentucky Colonel has been around since 1813. The Kentucky Militia had just returned from a highly successful "War of 1812"campaign that resulted in control of the Northwest being returned to the United States. When the militia disbanded, Governor Isaac Shelby commissioned Charles S. Todd, one of his officers in the campaign, as an aid-de-camp on the Governor's staff with the rank and grade of Colonel. Todd returned the favor a couple of years later by marrying Shelby's youngest daughter.

The first Colonel, Charles S. Todd

Early Colonels actually served military roles. In the latter part of the 1800's the position took on a more ceremonial function. In the late 1920's a group of Colonels started talking about forming a "society." Governor Flem Sampson gave his blessing. At the first formal meeting of the society in May of 1931, the Governor challenged the Colonels to "more closely band together this group into a great non-political brotherhood for the advancement of Kentucky and Kentuckians." And they did. Minutes of the early meetings confirm that charitable programs were to be a central part of the organization. Social events would also play an important role.

The opportunity for the Order to have a major impact on the state rained down in 1937. The Great Flood of 1937 was disastrous for the state. Kentucky Colonels from across the country chipped in to help the recovery. New York-based Colonels collected five dollars from each member. In California, Colonels such as Fred Astaire held benefits to raise money for Kentucky.

Recreation room for soldiers in training at Fort Knox during World War II—paid for by the Kentucky Colonels.

Kentucky Colonel Bing Crosby

Recovery from the flood was still ongoing as the war in Europe broke out. As WWII loomed at the change of the decade, the pockets of Kentucky Colonels were again tapped. The money raised was used to set up recreation rooms for soldiers in training at Fort Knox. Kentucky Colonels also set up and staffed the WAC recruiting office in Louisville.

The charitable side of the Honorable Order grew rapidly following the war. In 1946, Colonels pledged money to help start the Kentucky "Country Doctors" fund. Today the fund is known, more politically correct, as the "Rural Kentucky Medical Scholarship Fund" and has helped educate over 600 physicians who serve rural Kentucky.

Kentucky's first cancer treatment center and the Lions Eye Research Center also continue to serve Kentucky. Kentucky Colonels played a major role in funding both centers.

Colonels continue to contribute dollars to the goal of benefiting Kentucky and Kentuckians. The annual amount granted to Kentucky educational and charitable organizations passed the one million dollar mark in 1990.

Kentucky Colonels provided major funding for the Lions Eye Research Center.

Kentucky's first cancer treatment center was funded in major part by the Kentucky Colonels.

Someone in every county in the state has been touched by a program funded by the voluntary contributions of Kentucky Colonels living in every state in the nation, as well as Colonels living in nearly two dozen nations abroad.

Visit www.kycolonels.org to learn more about the Honorable Order of Kentucky Colonels. Indeed, we are known for our social events at Derby Time. However, our real purpose is to serve Kentucky as Ambassadors of Good Will and to adhere to Governor Sampson's directive. Today we state it this way: Kentucky Colonels Care.

No. | No.

Royal Crown Cola

Senior Guard
Hammie Davidson

Senior Guard
James Whitney

e Sweatt

Contents

FOREWORD

How do you cover over a century of Kentucky's rich basketball history in four or five hours of television? That's easy; you don't. As an independent filmmaker recruited by Kentucky Educational Television to produce a multi-part documentary series that covers girls and boy's high school basketball, women and men's college hoops, and even the professional ranks, I knew that my only hope would be to create a series of segments that could represent the larger picture. *Basketball in Kentucky: Great Balls of Fire* succeeds on that level.

Many of the state's hoops legends appear on camera: Basil Hayden, Geri Grigsby, Wah Wah Jones, Darrell Griffith, Joe B. Hall, Donna Murphy, Travis Grant, Rick Pitino, King Kelly Coleman and Ralph Beard, just to name a few. In all, over 250 on-camera interviews were conducted over a two-year period, making this project the most comprehensive collection of Kentucky basketball history ever assembled.

Filmmaker Tom Thurman interviews Freddie Maggard at Carr Creek gym for his documentary Basketball In Kentucky: Great Balls of Fire.

Many people long since departed are covered as well: Adolph Rupp, Uncle Ed Diddle, and Peck Hickman are among them, men who cast long shadows over the game's history. And then there are those who never made it into the show, or who were interviewed but ultimately not utilized. These untapped resources—combined with the massive archives of still photographs, game films and assorted memorabilia that was gathered—can someday provide future historians, filmmakers, writers, sociologists and even anthropologists with an abundance of materials that will supply the groundwork for additional exploration and study.

Thurman with S.T. Roach, legendary former coach of Dunbar High School in Lexington.

For the present, though, there is *Hardwood Heaven: Basketball In Kentucky.* The idea to create a book to accompany the television series was greeted warmly for it would provide another opportunity—in another medium—to shed more light on a topic held dear by so many Kentuckians. Why the need for yet another book on basketball in this basketball-crazed state? That's simple: while other volumes tend to focus upon a specific school, *Hardwood Heaven* takes a much broader view, infusing the subject matter with a sense of style and creativity often lacking in other documentations of the sport. Much more than simply a companion piece to the television series, this book stakes out its own territory, and captures the spirit and breadth of the game in a manner that will please the most knowledgeable of fans, and intrigue the most cynical.

Basketball in Kentucky is much more than a game with historical or sociological importance, though; it's downright personal. As the son of a high school athletic director here in Kentucky, I grew up with the game. My winter and early spring evenings in the 1960's and 1970's often consisted of accompanying my father to high school basketball games, beginning with the junior varsity tip-off around 6:30. After both games were finished around 10:00, my father began his final rounds—visiting with coaches, referees and fans, overseeing the cleanup of the gym, and making sure that all returned to normal in the then-quiet hall. I often remained long enough to sneak into the manager's storage room to secure a ball, return to the court, and attempt to recreate some of the moves I had witnessed that night, the solitary echo of the ball I dribbled reverberating through space that only a short time before had been filled with thunderous noises, sweat, and the dreams of players, coaches and fans alike. It was a great place and time in my life; too bad I wasn't worth a damn at playing the sport.

Much of what interested me took place far off the court. The games provided a social arena for kids and adults alike, and the seating arrangements offered a social microcosm of the entire community. The cheering section was reserved for high school students only, led by the off-court elite group: cheerleaders.

Pulitzer Prize-winning author Dave Kindred, former columnist for the Louisville Courier-Journal *and a longtime observer of the basketball scene in Kentucky, is the author of* Basketball: The Dream Game In Kentucky *(Data Courier, 1976).*

Parents and hard-core fans usually sat in the same spot game after game, and no stranger—especially an opposing fan—dare encroach upon this unstated territorial claim. The upper section was filled with those wanting more anonymity—silent and indifferent fans, those attending out of duty not passion, detached observers with less at stake, hormone-driven youngsters seeking out those spots with limited lighting to pursue other interests, and former athletes who came to watch what they used to be and often never were.

I was drawn repeatedly to the trophy case in the lobby, which was surrounded by framed articles from newspapers that documented the program's past glories. Most of all, I was interested in our school's 1966 state championship run, and I loved to read how that team marched through those four glorious rounds to win the ultimate prize: state champion of the Boy's Sweet Sixteen. For a ten-year-old boy, that accomplishment was greater than any Pulitzer or Nobel Prize or Academy Award. I was fascinated by the scores of the games, and by the teams that we beat—names like Central City and Knox Central and, of course, Male. And if the current team made it back to the Sweet 16, you could count on school being dismissed—the ultimate statement on the balance between school and athletics—for that glorious trip to Freedom Hall in Louisville. There, the KHSAA program held the magic for me. The historical data listed in the back intrigued me: teams that returned year after year (like Owensboro), teams that made it once never to return (like Bagdad), players like King Kelly Coleman, Linville Puckett, Howie Crittenden, Cliff Hagan, Butch Beard, and Wes Unseld; coaches like Bill Harrell, Morton Combs, William Lee Kean, Ralph Carlisle, and Robert Graves. After these interests were stirred as a youngster, it was with great anticipation when—over 30 years later— I was hired to produce a documentary series on the history of the game in Kentucky, affording me the pleasure of working with many of the very people I had so long idolized from afar.

The following is a Whitmanesque catalogue of favorite moments from the basketball project, submitted from one basketball fan to another:

1) Bill Keightly ("Mr. Wildcat") throwing me the oldest basketball he had and encouraging me to shoot around at my leisure in Memorial Coliseum, The House That Rupp Built;

2) Attending the annual reunion "on the hill" at the old Carr Creek gym, complete with former players, coaches, fans and cheerleaders;

3) Visiting the grave of Adolph Rupp with my children after the completion of the project on a sunny March morning;

4) Running into John Will "Scoop" Brown at the Sweet 16. When asked if he would grant me an interview, he said: "I took a pain pill this morning, so I feel alright. Let me put my teeth in and I'll be right there."

5) Visiting with Basil Hayden at his home in Mobile, Alabama, where we watched the Georgia Tech game together, a school that he had played against over 80 years earlier;

6) Cajoling Vernon Hatton into reciting a listing of all 38 UK All-Americans in an auctioneer's chant;

7) Talking Rick Pitino into singing the end of "My Old Kentucky Home."

8) Visiting the Blackburn-Ward funeral home in Versailles that featured a Wildcat coffin;

9) Transporting former Berea College player Irvine Shanks via limousine to the premiere at the Kentucky Theatre in downtown Lexington;

10) Interviewing my father.

None of these experiences were possible without the support and hard work of the following: Michael Kelsay (writer); Robert Booth and Marilyn Myers (associate producers); Craig Cornwell (executive producer); Mary Ann Carpenter (graphics coordinator); Otis Ballard (editor); The Honorable Order of Kentucky Colonels (sponsor); Michael Follmer (videographer); Gary Moseley (audio supervisor); my wife Lynn Motley and my parents, Arnold and Jeanette Thurman. My sincere and eternal thanks to you all.

And let us not forget those we have lost since this project began: Luster Oxley, Jim Calhoun and Scoop Brown. You are all sorely missed.

Tom Thurman
July 28, 2002

INTRODUCTION

by Dave Kindred

EVERY WINTER FOR 11 YEARS AS A COLUMNIST for the Louisville *Courier-Journal*, I drove around Kentucky in search of basketball stories. Some search. Like searching for stars in a clear night sky.

I found Joe Begley outside his general store along Letcher County's KY 7. A country philosopher and fierce opponent of strip miners defiling mountains to rip out coal, Begley had an idea about basketball's place in Kentucky. "If a lump of coal ain't Jesus Christ," he said, "basketball is." He meant that as an insult, though he said it with a rueful smile because he knew it worked both ways.

But let's stop short of saying Kentuckians worship the game. It's enough to say they love it. At Paintsville, a star forward on the high school team told me he perfected his one-on-one moves by working on a dirt court against his dog, Brutus, a Labrador retriever.

After I did a column predicting an Indiana University victory over Kentucky, a man in Berea sent me a sandwich bag filled with a dry, brown substance. "This is pure bluegrass horse manure," he said, "the same thing your article was made up of."

And Hazel Porter, Hazel Porter, dear, dear Hazel. Our 25 years as friends began before I met her. One day's mail brought a steaming letter from Hazel Porter of Frankfort, who identified herself as a UK fan upset with something I'd written. "If I ever see you," she wrote, "I'm going to hit you in the face with a pie." To which I replied, "Make it chocolate cream."

Stories galore, thick as stars. I drove thousands of miles, through mountain hollows and across barren flatlands, always on the lookout for the piece of metal sculpture that should be Kentucky's official symbol: a basketball hoop.

Hoops were everywhere, fashioned from coat hangers, barrel rings, and bicycle wheels. They were nailed to trees, garages, telephone poles, work sheds, great white mansions, and a dog house in Hardinsburg.

They came with new nets, no nets, ripped nets, nets of chain, nets of braided rope, red-white-and-blue nets, just plain nets. Anyway, who needs nets? Ralph Beard's mother said her son, the greatest guard in Kentucky history, got his start throwing a rubber ball into his potty chair.

Such datelines: Paintsville, Red Fox, Red Bird, Inez, Pippa Passes, and Betsy Layne . . .Burnaugh, Wurtland, Turners Station . . .Dawson Springs, Pinckneyville, and Jackson (where a funeral home raised a hoop next to the hearse's parking spot). . . Wayland and Glasgow and Hazel Green. . . Corbin, Carr Creek, and Lawrenceburg (where Rhoda Kavanaugh started her own school and attended games wielding an umbrella should a player need coaxing). . . Egypt and Mummy and Cairo and Monkeys Eyebrow.

Basketball everywhere—except in Balltown where a counterman at Bryant's Grocery said, "Naw, wasn't named for basketball as far as I know. A family named Ball settled here. The town's about 150 years old, and I don't think basketball was that important back then."

With its small, poor, rural towns, Kentucky came naturally by basketball, a simple game requiring neither many people nor much money. Every Kentuckian's hands know the tingly feel of a basketball. We love the rainbow arc of a jump shot from 20 feet. To run a fast break is to run free on the wind.

A simple game. And more. It gets in your heart. Maybe in Kentucky more than anywhere, maybe because Kentuckians needed it more than anyone, maybe because basketball success energized hundreds of small towns even as it did big towns, the game became a source of pride shared by people with few other things to share, certainly few so happy.

The game is everywhere, even underground. In St. Joseph there was an underground furnace room transformed into a gym 10 feet wide and 20 feet long. Steam pipes criss-crossed in the air two feet above the players' heads. As to why St. Alphonsus

16

Grade School created the gym, Father Walter Hancock said, "Basketball players make better grades."

Wade across Hell for Certain Creek in Leslie County, near Hyden and nothing else, you'll be deep in the shadowed recesses of Daniel Boone National Forest. There Amos Osborne built a recreation center, half of it a basketball court. Did he ever think of leaving out basketball? "Nope. The kids love it."

Down that way, too, was Kingdom Come High School, a three-story sandstone building with a gym on the second floor. A stove stood in one corner. Chicken wire covered windows to keep balls in the building. I asked Kingdom Come's star, Junior Halcomb, what it was like to play there. "It's hay-ul, man," he said.

Hay-ul, let's go to prison. At the Kentucky State Penitentiary near Eddyville, the man in charge of a league for 120 inmates said basketball worked wonders: "The boys in basketball don't have anything to do with the low morals of penitentiary life, the robbing and beating. You don't find basketball boys with home-made daggers or pipes, that sort of stuff."

We could sit in Memorial Coliseum with Adolph Rupp at an afternoon practice in the great man's 70th year of life, sitting in silence as he nods off to sleep. "Damn basketballs, bouncy, bouncy, bouncy," he said, suddenly snapping awake. "The legislature should pass a law that every day at 3:30 any coach who's 70 years old gets a shot of bourbon and a nap."

We must go back to the steaming letter-writer Hazel Porter. The week after she wrote to me, I leaned against a courtside railing. I felt a tap from behind on my right shoulder. A woman said, "Mr. Kindred?" I turned, and everything went dark. I suppose that generally happens when someone shoves a pie plate in your face. I reported the pie-ing with one lament: "It wasn't chocolate cream. It was shaving cream."

Maybe a month later, a small woman bubbling with feisty energy introduced herself.

"I'm Hazel Porter," she said.

I said, "The pie lady?"

"Oh, no, I didn't do that," she said.

For 25 years we left it there and in those 25 years I came to think of Hazel as the incarnation of basketball in Kentucky. She'd been a player herself, at Liberty in the late 1920s and early '30s. She told our mutual friend, the Lexington sports columnist Chuck Culpepper, "I used to dive onto the floor for the loose balls. I was good."

Did I say feisty? She once offered her glasses to a referee. At the Tennessee border, she used a guest register to tell the day's Vol coach, "Boo, Ray Mears." She carried a referee doll and, in sight of the striped incompetents, pulled off its limbs. Culpepper saw on her fireplace mantel a voodoo doll with pins through the photo of a Cincinnati columnist who'd disrespected the Cats. (Ouch. Give me pie.)

"The Meadowlands, 1996, was the first time she went to a Final Four with the Cats," says her daughter, Patti Porter. "As she stood in the parking lot, 79 years old, she just started crying, she was so happy."

Her home in Frankfort was a UK shrine, Big Blue souvenirs everywhere, even a lifesize cutout of Rick Pitino in the foyer. "At the end of every season," her daughter says, "she went into mourning. After a couple weeks of that, she began the countdown to Midnight Madness."

Hazel died in March of 2001. She was 84. A state legislature resolution in her honor declared "the passing of Hazel G. Porter has left a void that cannot be filled, and she is mourned across the length and breadth of the Commonwealth."

At Hazel's memorial service, the pastor finished his eulogy and stepped back. A moment of silence. "Then,

The UK seniors—G.J. Smith, Jerry Hale, Jimmy Dan Conner, Bob Guyette, Kevin Grevey, and Mike Flynn—savor their big win over Indiana, 92-90, in the 1975 Mideast Regional.

a crackle in the air," Culpepper wrote. "And crowds cheering. . . ." The silence had given way to the music in Hazel Porter's life: the rousing UK fight song, and Cawood Ledford's radio calls of the Cats on the run in big games, and, finally, with the sweetest sounds the old man ever made, there was Happy Chandler's voice, the governor one more time singing "My Old Kentucky Home."

Since that day, Patti Porter has looked for her mother's UK sweater and that referee doll with removable limbs. She hasn't found them, and she has come to what every Kentucky basketball fan will recognize as a reasonable conclusion, which is, "Mom must have taken them with her."

"The thing about basketball in Kentucky is its incredibly unifying force. My grandfather is 78 years old, and he and I wouldn't necessarily have much in common but, by golly, we can always talk about the Cats or the Louisville game. And it's like that all across Kentucky. You go to Ashland, or Paducah, go into the house of the richest man in town, or a blue collar area, or the welfare office, and you can talk about basketball. People are passionate about it. They know they can converse. It's sort of the universal language."

—Mark Story, *Lexington Herald-Leader*

"... *it's the only major world sport that has an inventor.*"

~ IAN NAISMITH

RIGHT:
Basketball's inventor, Dr. James Naismith.

Origins of the Game

By the time the Civil War broke out in 1861,
baseball was already on its way toward staking its claim
as our national pastime. It was a pastoral sport, for a largely rural nation.

Industrialization came to the nation in the second half of the nineteenth century.
Our cities became bigger, louder and grittier. And football became a popular
spectators' sport. The rhythm of the game mimicked that of the factory floor,
as the teams clashed and huddled over and over.

But if baseball and football were nineteenth century games,
then basketball was the first game of the twentieth century. It valued not only
speed and strength, but also placed a heavy emphasis on style and improvisation.

Like the quantum theory of physics or jazz music,
basketball is about acceleration, with grace and uncertainty.

It's about going to a place that, only a moment before, no one even knew existed.

And no one knew basketball existed until Dr. James Naismith
dreamed it up one morning in Springfield, Massachusetts.

Dr. James Naismith drafts rules
for a new game he calls "Basket Ball."

Basket Ball.

The ball to be an ordinary Association foot ball.

1. The ball may be thrown in any direction with one or both hands.

2. The ball may be batted in any direction with one or both hands (never with the fist).

3. A player cannot run with the ball, the player must throw it from the spot on which he catches it, allowance to be made for a man who catches the ball when running at a good speed.

4. The ball must be held in or between the hands, the arms or body must not be used for holding it.

5. No shouldering, holding, pushing, tripping or striking, in any way the person of an opponent shall be allowed. The first infringement of this rule by any person shall count as a foul, the second shall disqualify him until the next goal is made, or if there was evident intent to injure the person, for the whole of the game, no substitute allowed.

6. A foul is striking at the ball with the fist, violation of rules 3 and 4, and such as described in rule 5.

7. If either side makes three consecutive fouls it shall count a goal for the opponents (consecutive means without the opponents in the meantime making a foul).

8. A goal shall be made when the ball is thrown or batted *into the basket* from the grounds and stays there, providing those defending the goal do not touch or disturbe the goal. If the ball rests on the edge and the opponent moves the basket it shall count as a

#2.

goal.

9. When the ball goes out of bounds it shall be thrown into the field, and played by the person first touching it. In case of a dispute the umpire shall throw it straight into the field. The thrower in is allowed five seconds, if he holds it longer it shall go to the opponent. If any side presists in delaying the game, the umpire shall call a foul on them.

10. The umpire shall be judge of the men, and shall note the fouls, and notify the referee when three consecutive fouls have been made. He shall have power to disqualify men according to Rule 5.

11. The referee shall be judge of the ball and shall decide when the ball is in play, in bounds, and to which side it belongs, and shall keep the time. He shall decide when a goal has been made, and keep account of the goals with any other duties that are usually performed by a referee.

12. The time shall be two fifteen minutes halves, with five minutes rest between.

13. The side making the most goals in that time shall be declared the winners. In case of a draw the game may, by agreement of the captains, be continued until another goal is made.

First draft of Basket Ball rules. Hung in the gym that the boys might learn the rules – Dec, 1891 – James Naismith 6-28-31.

LEFT & ABOVE:
The original draft of rules for "Basket Ball."
RIGHT:
Author of the rules, Naismith.

"He came to the United States when he was 29 years old. He went to the Springfield YMCA, where they trained the directors … When he arrived, there was a need for a sport that could be played indoors, between football and baseball … And he kind of popped off a few times that he could invent an inside sport. So, actually, his boss, who was Dr. Luther Culick, said, "Well, it's time to put up or shut up. It's time to invent a sport." So Dr. Naismith actually intended to — and set off on a mission to — invent a sport. And he always said the first basketball game was played in his bed, the night before, because that's where it all came together.

He came downstairs, 11:00 in the morning, and had the stenographer type the original two pages of rules, which he had notes for, which is what we have with us today.

He was going to use boxes [for goals]. He visualized the goals being two 18-by-18 inch boxes. So when he came downstairs and gave his notes to the secretary, Miss Lyons, he said, "Type the notes. I only have 30 minutes before class."

He went to the janitor. "Mr. Stubbins," he said, "I need two 18-by-18 inch boxes for goals."

The janitor said, "I don't have boxes, but I've got two peach baskets in the basement. Will they work?"

And that's how it became basketball. It was very simple. And they played the first game December 31, 1891 — at 11:30 in the morning, in Springfield, Massachusetts, at the YMCA gym. And so it makes it a sport that's unique, because it's the only major world sport that has an inventor."

~ IAN NAISMITH

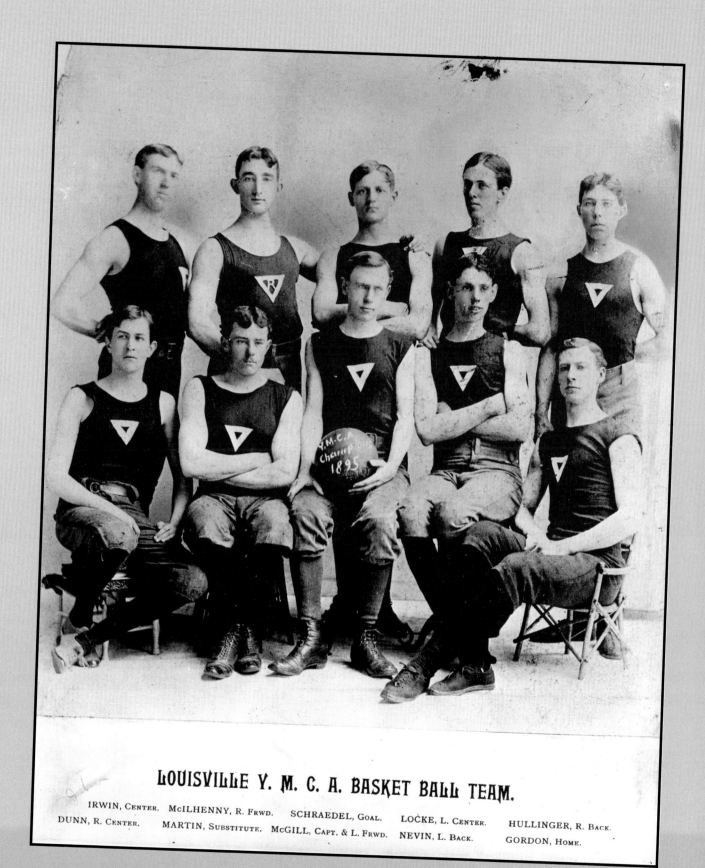

LOUISVILLE Y. M. C. A. BASKET BALL TEAM.

IRWIN, Center. McILHENNY, R. Frwd. SCHRAEDEL, Goal. LOCKE, L. Center. HULLINGER, R. Back.
DUNN, R. Center. MARTIN, Substitute. McGILL, Capt. & L. Frwd. NEVIN, L. Back. GORDON, Home.

ABOVE:
Louisville's YMCA team, 1895.

The first women's college basketball games in Kentucky are played.

1930-31   Left To Right: Isabelle Preston, Nancy Hurt, Alberta Young, and Lol. Scott.

RIGHT:

Four of the 1930-31 Ashland Kittens: Isabelle Preston, Nancy Hurt, Alberta Young, and Lola Scott.

"The earliest accounts that we have of womens' college basketball in Kentucky probably would start with a 1903 game between the University of Kentucky and Transylvania University. There were other colleges playing: Berea, Eastern, University of Louisville. In those early years, they had games, and when the Kentucky High School Athletic Association began to sponsor a state tournament for girls, then we do have some records of some outstanding teams — the Hazard team, the Woodburn team, Georgetown, the Ashland Kittens. They produced strong teams year after year, and were usually a part of the state High School Athletic Association's state tournament."

⁓ PEGGY STANALAND, HISTORIAN/AUTHOR

Early Women's Teams

"Our uniform was just bloomers. And then, our stockings came up above our knees. There was no skin showing. There was never any indication of it being illegal or indecent. My parents were very strict, in morals and decency, and they never objected to my playing basketball."

~ VIRGINIA "SHORTY" COMBS

Basketball had arrived at the tail end of the nineteenth century, and throughout the first decade of the twentieth, basketball teams were established from one end of the state to the other.

"My mother, Virginia Harris Combs, lived during the flapper period; but, of course, her father was a very strict person. And one year, she came home from college with her hair bobbed, and she thought he would probably disown her. But after he looked at her bobbed hair, he said, 'It will grow.'"

~ JAN TROSPER, DAUGHTER OF VIRGINIA "SHORTY" COMBS

ABOVE: *The University of Kentucky women's team was champion of its league in 1924.*

"The heyday of girls' high school basketball in the state of Kentucky, I think, was the 1920s decade. You know, we call it 'The Decade of the Flappers.'

I think that girls' basketball at the high school level in the 1920s was a reflection of the times. I think it was a reflection of the flappers' age. It was accepted. Mothers did not mind their daughters playing basketball. And, perhaps, some of their mothers had also played in the 'teens, because that was apparently a part of their upbringing. And so they didn't have an objection."

~ PEGGY STANALAND

The Kentucky High School Athletic Association put an end to the girls' state tournament in 1932. They would not play a state tournament game for 43 seasons.

"The Kentucky High School Athletic Association did not want to sponsor a state tournament for girls any longer, and they made that decision in 1932, shortly after the state tournament was over. And why that came about — there are some reasons—but I think it was a shock to most people as they read it historically.

Why? What happened? What did they do?"

~ PEGGY STANALAND

ABOVE: *The women's team from Centre College, ca. 1920s.*

BELOW:
The women of Olive High School, 1921.

"The official sanctioning of a state high school tournament did not mean the demise of girls' basketball in the state of Kentucky. They continued to play and, in fact — I think it was in the minutes statement of the High School Athletic Association — that it was okay if they wanted to keep playing one another in high schools, but there wouldn't be regional or district tournaments and no state tournament."

~ PEGGY STANALAND

"*I* don't know if we want to say that the higher-ups or administrators thought it was too rough of a sport for young women. It was not the, so to speak, 'in thing.' And there were enough individuals such as that that really became the stopgate. There weren't enough other individuals who would really come forward and say, 'We want this to continue.'"

~~ JOYCE SEYMOUR, GIRLS' LIT

BELOW: *A Kentucky team from 1913.*

ABOVE: Future coaching great Ed Diddle started by coaching the Western Kentucky women's basketball team. One of his forwards, Margaret Louise Monin (third from left) made the All State team, and later Diddle and she were married.

Diddle himself had been a star on the famous 1918 Centre College team that went 11-0, and counted on its roster John Sherman Cooper, Bo McMillin, Red Roberts and Madison Bell.

BELOW: At the same time Diddle coached Western's team, future governor, senator and Baseball Commissioner A.B. "Happy" Chandler coached the women's squad at the University of Kentucky. His players were (left to right) Margaret Ligon, Antoinette Harrison, Sarah Blanding, Thompson, and Elizabeth Carroll.

Beginning with Basil Hayden in 1921, the University of Kentucky has had 38 of its players selected for All-American honors, which is more than any other Division 1 school. Only three of those All-Americans—Hayden, Paul McBrayer and Carey Spicer—earned their honors before Adolph Rupp arrived in 1930.

Kentucky's Roaring 1920s

BASKETBALL

"I was the head basketball coach for the University of Kentucky in 1926. I took over the team just a week before the first game, so I wasn't able to get much coaching in. Besides, all the talent had graduated, so there wasn't much to work with, and there wasn't much chance of developing anything. Rupp was famous for winning, and I was famous for losing!"

~ BASIL HAYDEN
UK PLAYER, 1922
UK HEAD COACH, 1926

Basil Hayden (with ball) stands with his UK teammates after winning the first Southern Intercollegiate Basketball Tournament in 1921. William S. King (with trophy) hit the winning free throw in overtime to beat Georgia 20-19. This was the first significant victory in the history of Kentucky basketball.

"Basketball was rather primitive back in those days. The games were rough. It took a lot of contact before a referee would call a foul. Generally, the referees didn't know the rules, and you practically had to be knocked into the seats before they would call a foul."

~ BASIL HAYDEN

The UK team in 1925 (top to bottom): Captain Jimmy McFarland, Will Millward, Burgess Carey ("the star of the season"), Lovell Underwood, Foster Helm, Charlie Albers, and Charles Hughes. Center Karl Rohs is not pictured.

Boyle-Humphrey Gymnasium was the home of the Centre Colonels basketball team at the turn of the century, but was demolished for a new gym in 1912.

The 1929 Western Hilltoppers.

Tiny gyms, like this one at Centre College, were adequate for the relatively small crowds of the day, even at bigger schools like UK, Western and Eastern. The stands typically held a few thousand people at most, and came within inches of the court's sidelines. Basketball at this time was growing in popularity, but still paled in comparison to the fan interest and media coverage given to college football. It would soon grow in popularity in Kentucky with the success of Adolph Rupp at Kentucky and Ed Diddle at Western, along with the grass-roots interest of Kentucky high schools, which could afford a ball and a rim and could find five guys to make a team.

A team from tiny Carr Creek plays th

*P*rohibition brought the advent of bathtub gin and gangsters with Tommy guns. Tennessee tried a young teacher, as well as the theory of evolution, in the so-called "Scopes Monkey Trial," and the nation slipped into the Great Depression. The '20s also saw a sudden rise in the popularity of spectator sports. And by 1925 the Kentucky Derby was a national event. In 1928 a team from tiny Carr Creek High School, in Knott County, Kentucky, a team that played without the benefit of uniforms, a team that lost to mighty Ashland in the state tournament finals, was invited alongside Ashland to the national tournament in Chicago.

"The Carr Creek team was unusual, because they didn't have a gymnasium. They didn't have very sophisticated uniforms. All poor kids. They played on an outdoor court. And they played in the finals of the state tournament. That was very, very unusual."

❧ LUSTER OXLEY, FORMER BASKETBALL OFFICIAL

National Tournament in Chicago.

"When Carr Creek went to Richmond and won the tournament over there, that meant they were in the state tournament. They still were wearing the old clothes that they had made early in the season. So the Richmond fans put up enough money to buy them new uniforms for the state tournament."

~ DON MILLER, AUTHOR, *THE CARR CREEK LEGACY*

"In 1928, the Carr Creek team consisted of eight players. Only five played. They never called time out, and no one ever fouled out. Ashland didn't have any supporters. Everybody was for Carr Creek. They had turned away about 1,000 people. It [Alumni Gym] would only hold 3,800, here in Lexington. They put 4,000 people in there. And then the fire marshal made them leave. So a lot of people went over to the Kentucky Theater. So every few minutes, someone would phone the manager of the Kentucky Theater, and he would announce the scores."

~ DON MILLER

"The 1928 game — the state championship game between Carr Creek and Ashland — sort of put the state tournament on another level."

~ LUSTER OXLEY

The 1928 state and national champion, Ashland High. Ashland's star, Ellis Johnson, would go on to become a college standout with the University of Kentucky.

Kavanaugh High School

Rhoda Kavanaugh

By 1930 schools from the cities to the smallest towns, even the countryside, all had basketball teams, and some of the coaches of those teams made names for themselves— Western Kentucky's Ed Diddle made the jump from a high school in Greenville, Kentucky, and UCLA's John Wooden started his career at Dayton High in northern Kentucky. So sometimes the small rural schools produced winners. Whether they did or not, ever since Carr Creek's run in the '28 tournament Kentuckians love rooting for the tiny schools—the so-called Cinderellas, and Kavanaugh was frequently right there in the thick of it.

Rhoda Kavanaugh started the Anderson County school in 1903 as a prep school for young men seeking entrance to military academies, but it developed a strong reputation for turning out great basketball teams. Paul McBrayer, who coached at Eastern Kentucky; Ralph Carlisle, Lafayette's legendary coach; and Earl Jones, who led Maysville to the 1947 state championship, all had roots at Kavanaugh. And from 1928 to 1942 there was always at least one Kavanaugh graduate playing on the Kentucky Wildcats basketball team.

"She would go out to the floor during the games and stand beneath the basket with that umbrella and holler... every time they'd come down to her end, she'd say just one thing—'Boys, get that ball!' And if somebody got close to her, and she didn't think they were doing quite as well as they should, she'd reach out and tap them with the umbrella, and there was, you know, a lot of people that had problems with that, especially opposing coaches."

~ BILL KEIGHTLEY, UK BASKETBALL STAFF,
KAVANAUGH HIGH SCHOOL, 1945

Kavanaugh High School developed a strong reputation for turning out great basketball teams, players and coaches.

LEFT: *This Kavanaugh team featured young Paul McBrayer. Front row from left: Karl Toll, Paul McBrayer, Jimmy Hutchinson, Jerry Adkins, and Charles Vaughn. Back row from left: Hollis Ballou, Harry Towles, Leland Caldwell, Charles Boggess, and Coach Chidsey.*

"To get to the gymnasium she would have to come through our shower room where we changed clothes. And I mean she'd walk in there while we were changing or in the shower, and she'd always say, 'Boys, don't pay any attention to me, I'm nothing more than your mother,' and she'd just walk right on through, or sometimes she'd just stop and talk!"

∞ BILL KEIGHTLEY

Kavanaugh star Aggie Sale

"*F*orest Sale, of course, acquired the name of Aggie for obvious reasons. He was a farm boy, and he came to the university and majored in agriculture. You know, it has been conceded, privately, that Coach Rupp has stated that Aggie Sale was the greatest player he ever coached."

~ BILL KEIGHTLEY

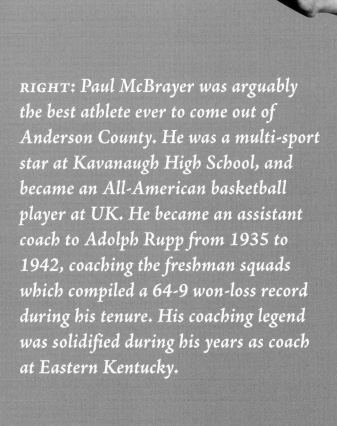

RIGHT: *Paul McBrayer was arguably the best athlete ever to come out of Anderson County. He was a multi-sport star at Kavanaugh High School, and became an All-American basketball player at UK. He became an assistant coach to Adolph Rupp from 1935 to 1942, coaching the freshman squads which compiled a 64-9 won-loss record during his tenure. His coaching legend was solidified during his years as coach at Eastern Kentucky.*

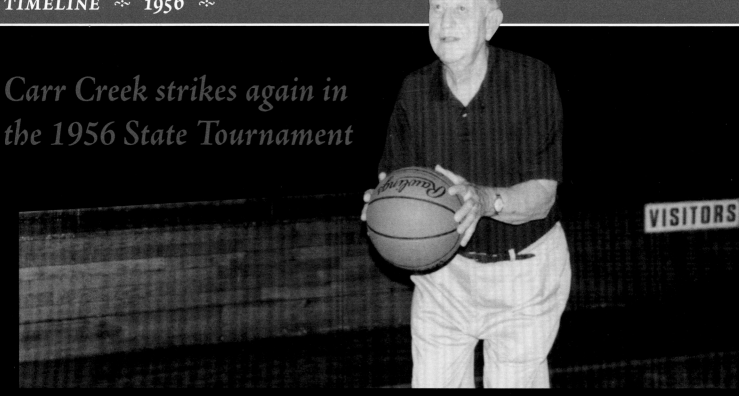

Carr Creek strikes again in the 1956 State Tournament

Coach Morton Combs at the Carr Creek gym, 2001. Carr Creek won the 1956 state championship, ending another captivating, improbable run to the title. As in 1928, when the Creekers came up just short, the 1956 team caught the imagination of the whole state.

"I remember so many incidents that you could talk about for hours...of the spots where I shot from and knew where every player was. E.A. was in the left-hand corner, Warren G's in the right-hand corner, Freddie's out front chewing his chewing gum, dribbling the ball. All these things are vividly imprinted on my mind."

—Jim Calhoun

What They Said—

in '28

Probably the best showing ever made by a small school in the national basketball tournament at Chicago was turned in by the team from Carr Creek, Ky. The entire enrollment of the school, for both the grammar grades and the high school classes, is only 194, but yet this team eliminated some of the best in the field and went as far as the quarter-finals.

in '30

Carr Creek returned to state in 1930 after the 1928 squad had downed Albuquerque, New Mexico, Bristol, Connecticut, and Austin, Texas, in national playoffs. Vienna, Georgia, pushed them out of competition by a 22-11 count in the national quarterfinals.

in '48

Those who survived the Male-Brewers bruising brawl with only minor heart palpitations should be full-fledged patients for the ticker experts after the Maysville-Carr Creek scramble.

The doughty Creekers had the defending champions on the ropes

Carr Creek took third place by defeating Male 47-41 in the consolation game.

The win was the Indians' second over the Purples this season, having won 42-40 in a season bout.

Will Rogers Writes About Carr Creek Basketball Aggregation

Will Rogers included in his Sunday paper article a long reference to the Carr Creek basketball team, of special interest to Greenville people because Miss June Ranney helped to start basketball in the Kentucky mountain school. Mr. Rogers' comment in his usual humorous vein follows:

"Well, sir, I guess you read about em. But if you have I must tell you more. The Carr Creek Basket Ball team, that kicked up such a fuss later on among all the best high school Basket Ball teams in America. They was in Lexington when I got there. They come from away down in the mountain. There is only 18 boys at their little country school. They played barefooted, and out on the ground. They just had the baskets fastened up to two trees, had no suits when they come to play in the Kentucky State Tournament. They walked in eight miles to get on the train, and it was one of those slow jerk-water lines, and the reporter in Lexington asked them how they made out coming from the Mountains, and the kid told em, "We made pretty good time till we got on the train." "The whole five is cousins and

two are brothers. They were [...] for the Kentucky Championship [...] one goal in I think it was the [sec]ond quarter. They never had [...] coach, and don't know what is commonly call by the coaches "[...] finger points of the game." The[y] just know one point, I don't kn[ow] if they call it fine or not, but the [...] is they have been told that the [...] of the game is to get that Ball [...] in that hoop, and Boy, how the[y] it! I think it's the greatest ex-ample of what any school [...] place can do. Its funny that [...] two greatest upsets in our Spo[rts] have been by Kentucky [...] when you think of what C[...] college at Danville did, a few yea[rs] back. I visited the school [...] they only have a couple of li[ttle] brick buildings, and to think the[y] beat Harvard; Then here are the[se] Kids right out of those Mountains beating big City teams from a[ll] over America. "The Carr Cre[ek] Boys!" That's a great kick to a[ny] country school any place, any-where to know that they can go outdo the principal sport just as good as any other school in Ameri-ca. "Viva Carr Creek!"

Up-to-Date Carr Creekers Have Brilliant 13-1 Record;

in '56

CARR CREEK may be a little backward when it comes to communications (there's no telephone in the community), but there's nothing backward at all about the Indians'

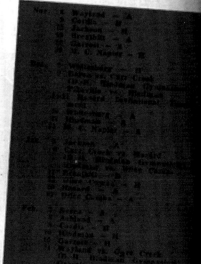

Torrid Carr Creek Runs String To 20;

school proud of its second team

We are very proud of our Second Team and rightly so.... They have a sensational record all their.... 16-0... Keep up the good work, fellows!!

Edward Watts - guard
Ray Stamper - forward
Carley Banks - guard
Hiram Amburgey - center
Eugene Massey - forward
Tyler Cornett - guard
Lewis Dean Cornett - guard
Marcus Combs - forward

Eugene Couch - guard
Jerry Kimberly - forward
W. B. Smith - guard
Corbett Mc Intosh - guard
Avary Ashley - guard
Vernon Pridemore - forward
Stanley Adams - guard
William Franklin - center

LEFT: *Coach Morton Combs walks the gym where so many happy memories reside, not just for him but for the entire community.*

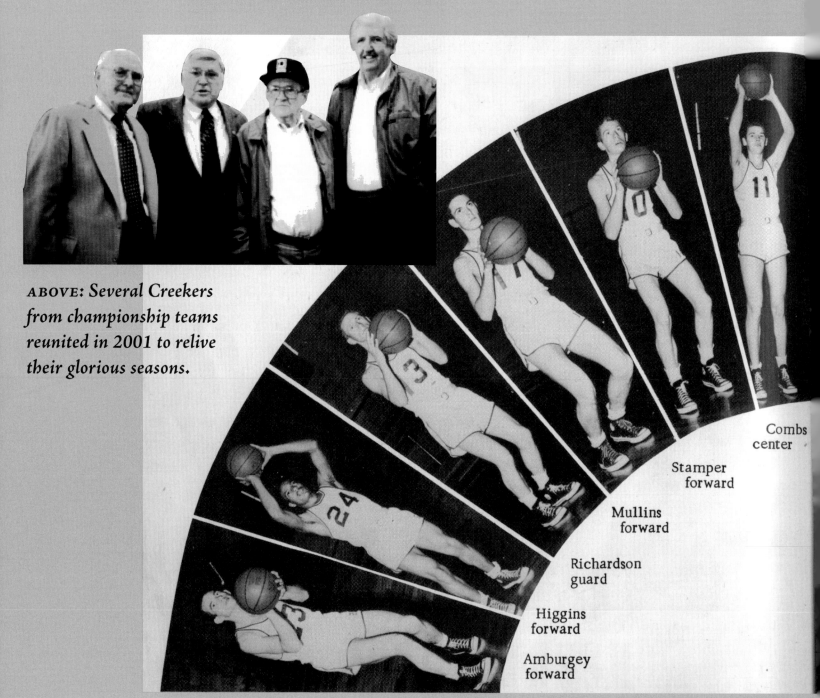

ABOVE: *Several Creekers from championship teams reunited in 2001 to relive their glorious seasons.*

Combs
center

Stamper
forward

Mullins
forward

Richardson
guard

Higgins
forward

Amburgey
forward

"I love the people here and love this place. Never a day passes that I don't reminisce...As I said, our roots...our heritage...is basketball."
—Marcus Combs

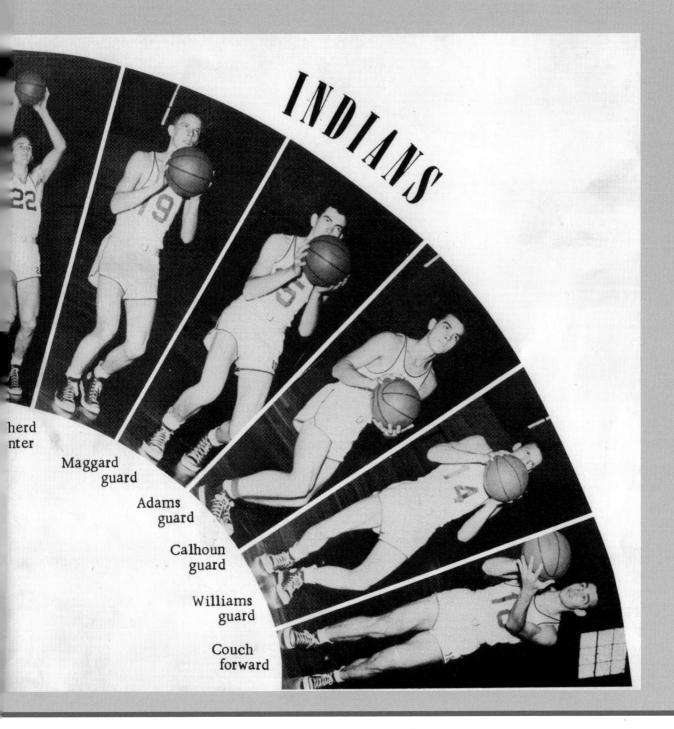

herd
nter

Maggard
guard

Adams
guard

Calhoun
guard

Williams
guard

Couch
forward

INDIANS

Adolph Rupp begins his University of Kentucky career.

In 1920, the University of Kansas had a scrawny young freshman on its squad — a young man who would fail to score a single point in his entire career as a Jayhawk. But he was an observant youngster who closely studied the game from the far end of the bench and learned all he could from the legendary Kansas coach, Phog Allen. And from one of Coach Allen's assistants, the man who invented the game, James Naismith. Following his graduation, that young man, Adolph Frederick Rupp, took what he'd picked up, first to Freeport High School in Illinois, and then, in 1930, on to the University of Kentucky in Lexington, where he would eventually win one NIT Championship and four NCAA titles. Rupp was fond of saying, "I won 876 games, and the boys lost 190."

Rupp's Early Years

"*M*y father was a multi-dimensional person. He was very smart. He was brilliant. As you probably know, he had his Master's degree from Columbia University."

~ "Herky" Rupp

"*N*o, I don't think I'm a dictator. I never was. I think I was rugged. I think I was firm. I don't think I was mean or any of those things that a lot of people think I was."

~ Adolph Rupp

LEFT: *More history here than in any one basketball photo ever taken. That's James Naismith, the mustachioed inventor of the game in the center, next to coach Forrest "Phog" Allen of the Kansas Jayhawks, and Adolph Rupp in the upper left corner. Rupp was a senior guard on Allen's undefeated Kansas team of 1923.*

"*C*oach Rupp was a smart man — really, really smart. A lot of people don't know this, particularly in New York. I said … I've asked those New York sportswriters — said, 'You know where he got his Master's?'

They said, 'Where? Kansas? Illinois?'

'No. Columbia University. You know, about ten blocks from where you work.'"

~ Earl Cox, Sportswriter

"Rupp did a lot of things for people that nobody ever heard about. And, you know, he liked … he loved children. And he was devoted to Herky, his son."

~ HUMZEY YESSIN, UK 1946–1949

"He was entirely different on the basketball floor than he was at home. I mean, he was a loving husband, a loving father, and a loving grandfather. And I'm not using the word 'loving' because I don't have a better vocabulary than that. That's what he actually was."

~ "HERKY" RUPP

"Everything he did was so repetitious. I mean, even the motels, the hotels we stayed in, they'd stayed in them 20, 30 years ago. I mean, he was just very superstitious."

~ MIKE CASEY

"I never had occasion to associate with him much off the court. I might tell you that I am and have been a teetotaler all my life, and Adolph wasn't, as you probably know. And so at Final Fours and so on we would be with different groups. But when I was with him in various clinics and so on, I always enjoyed him very much."

~ JOHN WOODEN

"I don't think people know the extent of his superstitions. But each year he handed down, from one set of managers to another, a booklet of superstitions, methods that had to be adhered to, that fit with his organization on game day.

And each morning, he'd get up on Andover Drive, and he would dress in the same procedure every game day. And that meant left sock, right sock, left shoe, right shoe, drive the same route to the Coliseum, park in the same place, eat the same pre-game meal. And he would walk back after the pre-game meal. There was a manhole cover on the sidewalk, across from the Coliseum, that he had to step on with his right foot before he crossed the street."

~ JOE B. HALL

LEFT: *Coach Rupp always insisted on a separation between himself and his players, like that between a general and his troops. At office hours he was always behind his desk, the CEO of the UK basketball company.*

"You could stop by the office. He had a secretary named Louise Gilchrist. And I'd go in there, and I'd say, 'Mrs. Gilchrist, could I see Coach Rupp for a few minutes?'

And she'd say, 'Well, let me go see.'

And the door would be open, and you could hear Coach Rupp say, 'Oh, my God, WHAT DOES THAT LITTLE TURD WANT NOW?'"

~ BILLY REED

> "As far as closeness with Coach Rupp, there was no closeness. There was a fine line. You stayed on your side, and he stayed on his. You didn't get familiar with him."
>
> ~ EARL "BROTHER" ADKINS

RIGHT: *Rupp's first UK team in 1930. The 29-year-old coach introduced a radical new system to the boys called the "fast break", and by the time the first game rolled around the 'Cats were in good enough shape to ring up 67 points to their opponent's 19. No UK team had ever scored more than 59 points in a game. After steamrolling through the regular season, the team was beaten in the Southern Intercollegiate championship game by Maryland on a last-second shot. Standouts on this team included All-Americans Carey Spicer (holding ball), Forest "Aggie" Sale (to his left), and Ellis Johnson in the middle of the top row.*

"Adolph was a larger-than-life character. He knew it. He played on it. He loved it.

He, one time, proposed that the rims be raised to twelve feet. I asked him once if he really believed that would make the game better. He said, 'Hell, no! But the guy needed a column, so I told him that.'

Bill Spivey once told me that Adolph wanted everyone to hate him.

And he succeeded."

~ DAVE KINDRED

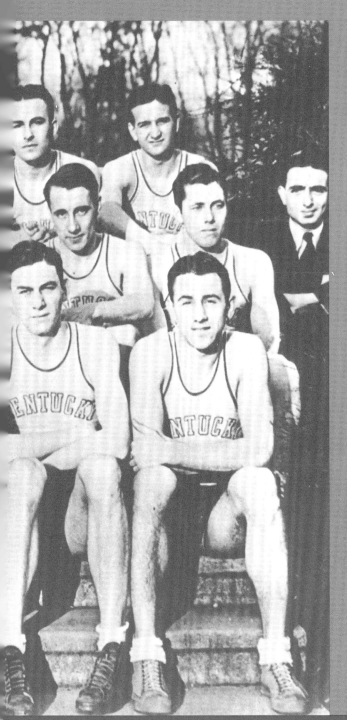

"He demanded everything to be the way he wanted it. He would not let any player talk unless he asked him something. And he had a saying that you can only talk if you can improve on silence."

~ EARL COX

"In those days, you only had two officials, and he'd fussed at a couple of them in the first half. And they came back out for the second half. He's sitting on the bench. The bench was at the end of the floor in those days. He's sitting in the middle of the bench, and the two officials came by, and he said, 'Fellows, I am a very sick man. I want you to sit down beside me, here, for just a minute. I'm a very sick man. And if I should die, I want to be like Jesus Christ — die between two thieves.'"

~ BILL KEIGHTLEY

"*You didn't challenge Coach Rupp. You didn't do your thing; you did his thing. And that was one of the things that set him apart—is that if he took a star player, they had to learn his system of play. He didn't adapt to the star player.*"

~ GUY STRONG

Adolph and Harry Lancaster were traveling on a recruiting trip down in Western Kentucky. And they were on their way home to Lexington, stopped in a restaurant and ate. And after they were done eating, Adolph went up to the cashier and asked if he could give them a check instead of cash. And the woman who was the cashier, she said, 'Well, of course, Mr. Diddle. You can give us a check anytime.'

And he left there. He was so chagrined. I heard that his buddy, Harry Lancaster, just had to cross his legs in the car going home to keep from laughing."

~ COTTON NASH

Ed Diddle begins a 42-season reign at Western

A former standout at Centre College who played alongside future U.S. Senator John Sherman Cooper, Diddle became Western's head basketball coach in 1922. In his first game, the Hilltoppers squad blasted its opponent 103 to 7. Afterward, Diddle said, "The people like to see scoring, and we give them what they like," which Coach Diddle continued to do for 42 seasons and 759 victories. And before it was over, both Diddle and Rupp would be inducted into the Basketball Hall of Fame. One of them would be known as "The Baron," the other as "Uncle Ed."

Western's "Uncle Ed"

"*I* think you will find, if you talk to players who knew Coach Diddle and eventually ended up playing for other coaches, you would find that they had a great affection for Coach Diddle. They loved him because of his interest in their welfare, because of his compassion for them as a student and a player. He was not just interested in what a player might do for him; he was interested in seeing them succeed, wherever they might be. And I think it sort of sets him apart from the attitude that some might have."

~ DR. DERO DOWNING

ABOVE: *Ed Diddle as the center and star player for the 1919 Centre Praying Colonels, considered the best team in the South.*
LEFT: *Kentucky legends— Uncle Ed and the Baron.*

ABOVE LEFT: *The 1947-48 Western team prepares to board their plane for New York City where they will play in the National Invitational Tournament in Madison Square Garden.*

ABOVE: *By the 1950-51 season, Western had long been established as a national basketball powerhouse, worthy of its own airplane.*

"*H*e was tough on you at practice, and he was tough on you at times; but, you know, he'd put his arm around you and he showed us all a lot of love. And you'd really play for a man like that."

~ DAREL CARRIER, WKU 1961

ABOVE: *As he did at every home game, Coach Diddle waves his red towel to the faithful.*

BELOW: *Diddle (seated, far right) holds court at the 1939 Kentucky Intercollegiate Athletic Conference.*

No. 622

This Dodge sedan was presented to Coach Diddle by WKU and the city of Bowling Green after the 1938 season, in which Western won the KIAC and Southern Intercollegiate basketball championships.

"He was a motivator. He could get you to play.
He could shed a tear just at the right time, you know
… I mean he, emotionally, could get to you. He could
also bless you out with the best of them."

~ BOB DANIELS, WKU 1957

"He loved to eat. He was a big eater. And it was told, at one point, that he went into Riley's Bakery and ordered this pie. And they said, "Would you like to have it cut into eight pieces, or four pieces?"

And he said, "Oh, cut it into four. I don't believe I could eat all eight."

~ DR. DERO DOWNING

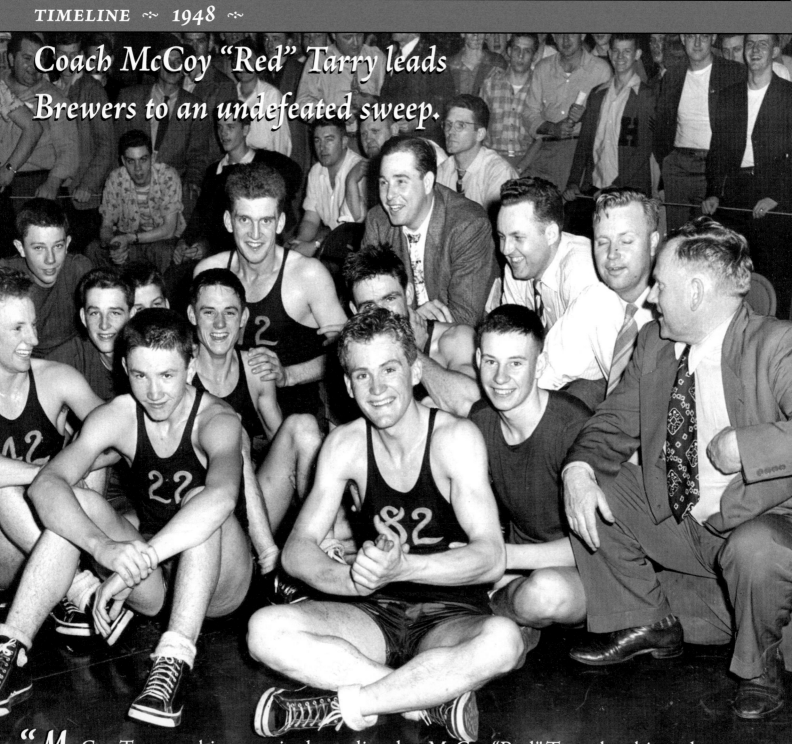

Coach McCoy "Red" Tarry leads Brewers to an undefeated sweep.

"McCoy Tarry . . . his name is always listed as McCoy "Red" Tarry, but his real name is Mark. And that's what his wife called him. That's what Barney Thweatt, who has turned out to be the historian of the team—that's what he calls him."

∾ EARL COX

Coach McCoy Tarry and Brewers

A David-versus-Goliath storyline is a compelling one for Kentuckians, who have consistently pulled for the underdog in state tournament play. In an amazing five-year span, from 1937 to 1941, the state champions were the Midway Bluejays, the Sharp Sharpshooters, the Brooksville Polar Bears, the Hazel Green Frogs, and the Inez Indians. But perhaps no small school will ever match the accomplishments of Coach McCoy Tarry's 1948 Brewers' squad. The Redmen, of the 73-student Western Kentucky High School, swept the regular season, won their district, their region, and then the state championship. Their final record was a glittering 36 and 0. And, more than a half a century later, Brewers remains the last boys' state champion to finish a season <u>undefeated</u>.

"You'd see a little, short, red-haired fellow; kind of hefty, sitting there with a towel he'd be chewing on. He'd have a bottle of water by his side. He'd be sitting on a bag of basketballs. He'd put about six in a bag. And, because he was so short, he couldn't be comfortable sitting on the bleachers or in a chair. He was more comfortable sitting on the balls."

~ BARNEY THWEATT

ABOVE: *Brewers outscored its opponents in 1948 by an average of 70 to 30.*

ABOVE RIGHT: *Coach Tarry and the boys admire their state championship trophies.*

"We were well balanced all year long—in fact,
the final game, I think all the first 5 scored from 9 to 19."

~ BARNEY THWEATT

"And they were a running team. They ran the whole game, up and down, zipped up
and down the whole game. And they were a entertaining team; played hard; never
gave up on a loose ball. And they were one of the teams responsible for that little
team out there that's always got a chance to win. And they did."

~ JOCK SUTHERLAND

Coach McCoy Tarry and the five Brewers starters in their patented circle. Brewers beat Letcher Norton's Clark County team, then Pap Glenn's Male team, then Maysville to win the state championship in 1948. Brewers was undefeated in 36 games.

"You have all the players lying on their stomachs on the floor, around a circle, whether it's the midcourt or foul lane. And Dad's there with them. They all have their arms around each other, and they're just getting ready to start the ballgame. Everyone's together. Everybody's on the same page. But—you could ask any of those players—you did not want to be the one that was beside Dad, especially on his right hand, because when Dad got up, he was going to smack somebody's tail with his hand and say, 'Let's go, Babe!' And that's what he would always say. 'Let's go, Babe!' And they would, and they did, that year."

~ MIKE TARRY
SON OF MCCOY TARRY

Rupp's Wildcats seize one title after another.

BELOW: UK's first national
championship came in 1946,
when this team won the NIT.

Wildcats' Winning Era

Nineteen-forty-six began a 13-season run that is the foundation upon which Adolph Rupp's legacy rests, after winning or sharing nine SEC titles and establishing a regional dominance in the South. In 1946, his Wildcat team won the NIT before a national audience — a team that featured freshmen and future All-Americans, Wah Wah Jones and Ralph Beard. Rupp's success extended into the 1950s, with two NCAA Championship teams that starred players such as Bill Spivey, Shelby Linville, Cliff Hagan, and Frank Ramsey on the '51 title team, and Vernon Hatton, Adrian Smith, and Johnny Cox for the 1958 champs.

But it was in the late '40s, with the team that came to be known as "The Fabulous Five," that Rupp had his best and most important run. Joining All-Americans Jones and Beard on the Fabulous Five were Cliff Barker, Kenny Rollins, and a third All-American, Alex Groza. This team won SEC championships every year, and NCAA championships in '48 and '49. This group of young men—Groza, Beard, Rollins, and Jones—made up half of the Olympic Gold Medal Team of '48, with Rupp serving as an assistant coach. They began their professional careers together, as both stars and owners of an NBA franchise created especially for them, the Indianapolis Olympians. But for all their Olympic and NBA glory, it is their run as Wildcats, from 1946 to 1949, for which they are best known.

"I think, in many ways, the Fabulous Five
had a lot to do with revolutionizing
the game of basketball and making it
more popular on a national basis."

~ BILLY REED

"Well, the Fabulous Five is, to me, the most unique group of college players to ever play the game, just simply because they won the NIT Championship...they won a couple of NCAA Championships...they represented the United States in the '48 Olympics, along with Philips Oilers, and won the Olympic Championship. And then, from that, with the help of Babe Kimbro and others, they go directly, as a unit, into what was then the NBA."

~ C.M. NEWTON

BELOW: *The UK coaching trinity for many years—coaches Adolph Rupp, Harry Lancaster, and Joe B. Hall.*

ABOVE: *The Fabulous Five—Ralph Beard, Kenny Rollins, Cliff Barker, Wah Jones, and Alex Groza—with the Baron.*

"It's amazing that today people go back and say something about the Fabulous Five. It's just a shame that Michigan tried to horn in on it, because of the 'Fab Five.' I say, 'Well, they weren't the Fabulous Five. We all graduated and they're still trying to.'"

WALLACE "WAH WAH" JONES

Groza screens, Beard shoots, Wallace Jones is in rebounding position.

Kenny Rollins

"Yeah, I could play basketball a little, and that's the only thing I ever really wanted to do. And, yeah, yeah, I could play the D—I could shut somebody down. I was cat quick. I could pass it. I could shoot it. Good Lord blessed me, that's all."

~ RALPH BEARD

"Kenny Rollins was our captain. He was already 25 years old...he'd been in the service, played at the Great Lakes Naval Training Station. He was really tough; he wasn't the best shooter in the world, but he didn't have to be. He was one of the best passers in the world. He started all our plays...a lot of times he sacrificed himself to let some of the other boys have the ball."

~ RALPH BEARD

"Cliff Barker could handle the basketball as well as anybody I have ever seen. He could twirl the ball on his hands and everything. He was a German P.O.W. for three years, but he always had a basketball with him."

~ RALPH BEARD

Cliff Barker

"Wallace Jones was a magnificently constructed man, big shoulders, strong, and had an innate ability to put the ball into the basket. He had the ability to hit one from the dead corner, which was really an unprecedented, hard shot."

~ RALPH BEARD

ABOVE: *Alex Groza*

"Groza—the ideal, unselfish, big man. He led our team in scoring all the time, because he was the hub of our offense; good passer also, unselfish. He could take the big guys out on the floor, and he was really only about six-six. They always listed him at six-seven, but he was about six-six. He'd take the big guys out on the floor and shoot over them. He was the consummate big man."

~ RALPH BEARD

Defensing Groza was a tough assignment, and overmatched centers used every tactic in the book, and a few that weren't in the book.

ABOVE: *Adolph Rupp collects his first NCAA Championship trophy in 1948 from Kenneth Wilson. The finals were held that year at Madison Square Garden in New York. Onlookers include John Stough, Joe Holland, Ralph Beard (behind the trophy), Wallace Jones, Kenny Rollins, Roger Day, Cliff Barker and Assistant Coach Harry Lancaster.*

"Bill Spivey was the kingpin. I mean, Bill was the first really mobile big player to come into college basketball. Here's a guy, seven feet tall… when we first saw him, I roomed with him as a freshman, and Bill was skinny as a rail. But, as he developed physically, and developed his game, he was much more than just a big man. He was a very skilled big man. He could shoot the hook shot. He could run like a deer. He could do all the things that you see modern basketball players do. But you didn't see that back then."

～ C.M. NEWTON

"Cliff Hagan was one of the most complete basketball players I ever saw, and he had the mark of greatness. You know, the great ones … Most guys go up and try to get a rebound, then try to come back down and go back up with it, or they'll flail at it on a tip-in. When Cliff went up and put his hand on the ball, it went in. He just had that knack."

~ GUY STRONG

RIGHT: *Minneapolis, 1951. Kentucky has just beaten Kansas State 68-58 to win the 1951 NCAA Championship, its third in four years. Celebrating are (kneeling): Lou Tsioropoulos, Bob Moore, C.M. Newton, Bobby Watson, Cliff Hagan, and Skippy Whitaker. (Standing) Trainer Smokey Harper, Walt Hirsch, Dwight Price, Bill Spivey, Guy Strong, Harry Lancaster, Adolph Rupp, Roger Layne, Shelby Linville, and Frank Ramsey.*

"Ramsey was the only player that Coach Rupp would allow to dribble the ball anytime that he wanted to dribble the ball. And he could take the ball and make all kind of moves. His famous move was a spin move, going one way, then make a quick pivot and go the other way. But he could hit the outside shot, he could drive, he could play defense. He was a complete ballplayer."

~ LOU TSIOROPOULOS

"Johnny Cox was a great corner shooter, and he was also one of those guys that has a way of attracting people to him. He has a charisma about him, and he was … nobody had seen anybody shoot that particular shot like he did."

~ JOCK SUTHERLAND

"They called him [Cox] 'The Kentucky Long Rifle.' He had a long, one-handed set shot that was deadly. He had to be deadly, 'cause when he was practicing in Hazard, in the hollows, if he missed, the ball would roll 500 or 600 yards down in the hollow, and he'd have to go chase it. So he wanted to make sure he hit that shot."

~ VERNON HATTON

LEFT: *In the 1958 NCAA Championship game, UK faced Seattle and its All-American (and future pro great), Elgin Baylor. Here the Cats have him surrounded with Johnny Cox (24), Don Mills (54), Vernon Hatton (52), and John Crigler (32). Kentucky won its fourth NCAA crown 84-72.*

The Fiddlin' Five win it all again in 1958, in Louisville's Freedom Hall.

RIGHT: *Vernon Hatton wears the net after winning it all in 1958. Hatton scored 30 points in the final, and later was named to the All-American team.*

"And, Rupp, of course, he wanted, and got, credit for putting a bunch of … he called us 'The Fiddlin' Five,' kind of making fun of us, not being the 'Fabulous Five,' who had won two national championships. But they always called it some kind of five. And we were the 'Barnyard Fiddlers' until we won that. And then we had thought that maybe we had turned into 'Carnegie Hall violinists.'"

VERNON HATTON

"And we got behind, but John Crigler started driving to the basket, and Elgin Baylor started fouling him. In fact, he got three quick fouls in the first quarter, and Baylor couldn't guard us; we kept pounding him. And Johnny Cox had 24 points. I had 30 points. Crigler had 13. We all contributed to the game and wound up beating Seattle for the National Championship in 1958, by the score of 84 to 72. I'll never forget cheerleaders pile-sacked us on the floor. They were all over me, and I was married at the time. And my wife kept pulling the cheerleaders off of me, 'Come out of there, Vernon!'"

VERNON HATTON

BELOW: *Cox, Crigler and Mills have a Seattle player pinned in the lane.*

ABOVE: *Rupp with three-time All-SEC player Billy Ray Lickert.*

BELOW: *After a few disappointing seasons, these two players, Cotton Nash (left) and Larry Pursiful (24) got the Cats back on a winning track in 1962.*

ABOVE: *Scotty Baesler was UK's starting guard for the 1961-62 season.*

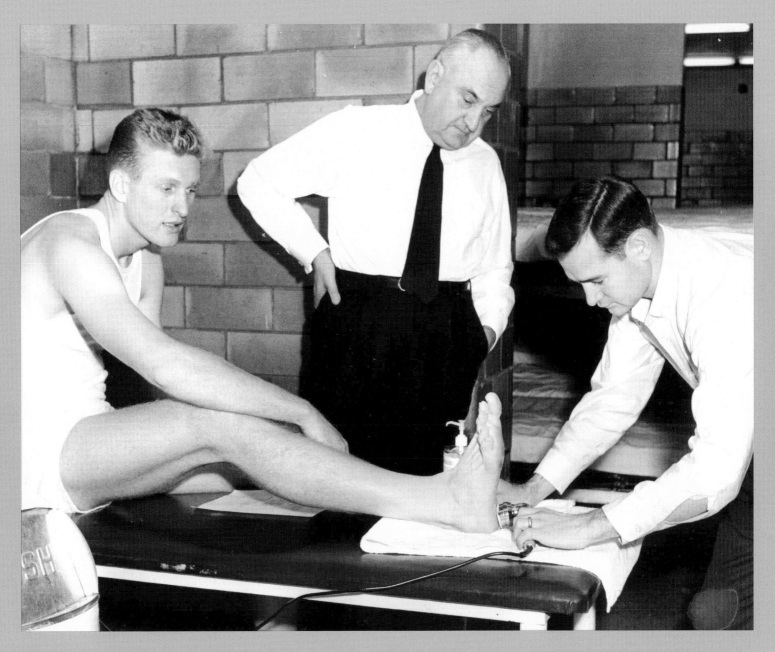

Cotton Nash led the SEC in scoring his first varsity season, 1962-63 (as a sophomore), and seemed to be the anointed one, the great redeemer of The Program, which had not been to the NCAA tournament since winning it in 1958. He got them there in 1964, but couldn't get past the first round. But before his career was over he became UK's all-time leading scorer (up to that time) with 1,770 points.

Segregated basketball produces history-makers.

"*M*ost of the coaches — in fact, all the coaches — just knew that they had teams superior to the Kentucky High School Athletic Association. But, because of the … what should I say — laws, here in Kentucky — black schools could not play white schools and, therefore, we had to use … have our own state tournament."

❧ S.T. ROACH

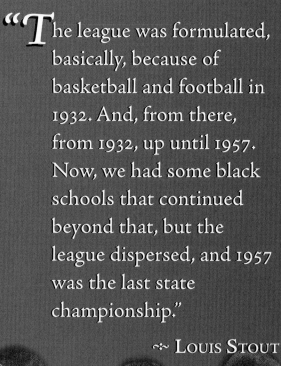

Senior Guard
Hammie Davidson

Senior Guard
James Whitney

"*T*he league was formulated, basically, because of basketball and football in 1932. And, from there, from 1932, up until 1957. Now, we had some black schools that continued beyond that, but the league dispersed, and 1957 was the last state championship."

❧ LOUIS STOUT

African-American Pioneers

Between 1932 and 1957 the Great Depression came to an end. The atomic bomb was developed and deployed, and the Allies won World War II. But African-American high school athletes in Kentucky played in a separate, segregated league: the Kentucky High School Athletic League, a counterpart to the all-white Kentucky High School Athletic Association. Many observers, at the time, felt certain that some of the KHSAL teams would have won the Sweet Sixteen had they been allowed to compete. William Lee Kean's Central High teams won the KHSAL title five times, and four times went to the national tournament in Nashville and came away champions.

Kean was not the whole show, however. At Lexington Dunbar S.T. Roach was making a name for himself. Following integration, Dunbar met the other city schools including Lafayette, coached by Ralph Carlisle, whom Adolph Rupp called "Kentucky's Greatest High School Coach." And Carlisle's record speaks for itself. His Lafayette Generals won state championships in 1950, 1953, and again in 1957. His lifetime record was 488 wins against only 144 losses. Even so, it's been said that Carlisle left coaching because he grew tired of losing to S.T. Roach and his Dunbar teams. The KHSAL featured a number of great coaches in addition to Kean and Roach. There were, among others, Newton Thomas at Horse Cave, J.G. Fletcher at Richmond, Frank Moxley at High Street School in Bowling Green, and another coach in Lexington, Charles Livisay at Douglass.

"We had the realization that we could defeat any of those white schools in the state tournament. But we knew what the situation was, so we just lived with the conditions we had to play under."

~ S.T. ROACH

"We told our boys in the [illegible] 'You are [illegible]. Anything you do that's [illegible] the rules and [illegible] of the game will be detrimental [illegible] the black participation. So let's conduct ourselves aboveboard.'"

~ S.T. ROACH

LEFT: *Coach Frank Moxley of High Street School in Bowling Green.*

ABOVE: *The Sweet Sixteen in the early 1960s at Memorial Coliseum in Lexington features a game between black and white high schools, still a relative rarity here, five years after KHSAL teams were allowed into the Kentucky High School Athletic Association.*

LEFT: *Charles Livisay with members of one of his Lexington Douglass teams.*

"Coach Roach was an absolute gem and would have to go down as one of the very best of all time."

~ JOCK SUTHERLAND

BELOW: KHSAA President Louis Stout with Coach S.T. Roach. Roach's Lexington Dunbar teams won 512 games, losing 143, from 1942 to 1965.

ABOVE: *Coach Willie Lee Kean (center).*

"Willie Lee Kean was one of the best all-around coaches. He coached football, basketball, and track. Central, every year, had some tremendous ballplayers under Mr. Willie Kean."

~ JOHN "SCOOP" BROWN, BASKETBALL OFFICIAL

RIGHT: *Coach Kean (third from left) with other coaches from the KHSAL. Kean coached at Central from 1923 to 1956, compiling an astonishing 857-83 record. During that span his teams played in the KHSAL finals 10 times, winning it 5 times. But he never got to coach in the regular State Tournament, from which black teams were excluded until 1957. Louisville Central finally won the State in 1969 with coach Bob Graves, beating Ohio County 101-72.*

"Without a doubt, Central High School, under the leadership of Coach Kean, not only in basketball but in the sport of football, was the echelon of high school for African Americans. I mean, they were *the* school."

~ LOUIS STOUT

"Coach Roach ... one of the finest coaches I've ever known. He was a real disciplinarian. Believe it or not, Coach Roach was a disciplinarian, but everybody had a fair chance to start on his team. If you produced in practice, you started. He had no pets. And Coach Roach is probably one of the finest men that I've ever met."

~ HERB WASHINGTON
DUNBAR HIGH SCHOOL, 1959

ABOVE: *A KHSAL CHAMPIONSHIP TROPHY.*

"If anybody is deserving of being in the Kentucky High School Athletic Association Hall of Fame, Newton Thomas has to be there. And I'm hoping that can be done before his time is up, here on Earth, because he is a pioneer. When you talk about Newton Thomas you probably talk about the godfather of adversity, relative to what he had to come through, what he had to deal with, and how he survived it."

~ LOUIS STOUT

LEFT: *Coach Newton Thomas*

"*I*n the early 1960s I was on the high school beat for the Lexington *Leader* which, then, was the afternoon paper in town. And I was, if not the first, one of the first white reporters to go to Dunbar to actually cover games there.

I could remember one night, though, when I came back to the office and the city editor came up to me and said, 'What games you cover tonight?'

And I said, 'I covered Dunbar and Male.'

And he said, 'What are you, some kind of a n____ lover?'

And I said, 'No, sir. It was just the best game in town, that's all.'"

~:~ BILLY REED

RIGHT: *Dotson High School, 1943.*

Dotson Basketeers Have Enviable Record

Above is shown the 1943 Dotson High School basketball squad which has won all home games this season except one. Pictured with them is the Dotson queen, Mary Helen Rice. Players are: No. 18, Rice, captain; No. 99. Boyd; No. 48, Shortt; No. 33, Eisen; No. 77, R. Morse; No. 25, Street; Principal E. R. Hamilton and Coach H. V. Smith. Dotson | No. 65, Smith; No. 30, C. Morse; has defeated the teams of Madisonville, Hopkinsville, Bowling Green, Henderson, Earlington, Providence and Brookport, losing only to Paducah on the local floor.

"I just wonder how many of those great players could have made U of L so much better, Kentucky so much better, if they could have just played."

~ EARL COX

"*If* you look at Newton Thomas, you look at S.T. Roach, you look at Carl Helem, you look at Coach Kean before he passed; these guys were the history makers."

~ LOUIS STOUT

ABOVE: *Coach Kean with one of his Central teams.*

RIGHT: *Coach S.T. Roach*

LEFT: *Grant High School.*

The Harlem Globetrotters become an influence in tiny Cuba, Kentucky.

Howie Crittenden could dribble, but he could pass, too—here against Corbin.

Cuba High School

*F*our years after Brewers' 1948 title run, another high school team emerged from the western end of the state, in tiny Cuba, from the Jackson Purchase area of far western Kentucky. Two boys, named Howie Crittenden and Doodle Floyd, fell under the influence of Marques Haynes and Goose Tatum, of the famed Harlem Globetrotters. They even convinced the team to warm up to the strains of Sweet Georgia Brown. And when their time came, they proved they not only knew how to put on a show but how to win.

*"O*nce I saw Marques Haynes and his dribbling... I had never seen that. We had never seen anything like the Globetrotters. In fact, I didn't even know that there was a team called the Globetrotters, to be honest about it. But when I saw Marques Haynes and his dribbling, I knew I wanted to learn how to do that."

~ HOWIE CRITTENDEN

107

"And I think, at halftime, the score was 30 to 24, I believe. And when they went in for their halftime break, they all were looking to Coach Story to say some magic words to them. But instead, Coach Story just said, 'This is the last time that you will play together. You've played together for five years, and this is the very last time that you're going to ever play together.' So he said, 'You just do what you will,' and he turned and walked out …"

~ MARIANNE WALKER

DOODLE
FLOYD

"… once Cuba got ahead, there in the last few minutes, last few seconds, Howard got the ball. And, of course, once he got the ball, he could keep it as long as he wanted it. And he could dribble that ball where nobody could get it. And Manual just could not get their hands on the ball."

~ MARIANNE WALKER

"The time that Doodle and I played in 48 years ago at Cuba High School, a small school—those days are over in Kentucky because we've had so many consolidations. The day of the small school coming up and winning the state tournament is going to be even more of a miracle, because you don't have the small schools like you used to."

~ HOWIE CRITTENDEN

COACH STORY AND HOWIE CRITTENDEN BRING THE 1952 STATE TROPHY BACK TO CUBA, RIDING ON THE BACK OF A CONVERTIBLE.

Ralph Beard and Alex Groza are implicated in a point-shaving scandal.

"The night they locked me up, in the Cook County Jail, January 21, 1951, if it's hell, if I'd had a snub-nosed revolver, I wouldn't be sitting here talking to you. I'd have killed myself. Now, you know, that may sound melodramatic, but, by God, that's the truth."

❧ RALPH BEARD

RALPH BEARD WAS QUICK, FAST, AND COULD USE EITHER HAND.

Kentucky Basketball on Trial

Change was the hallmark of the years from World War II through the 1950s. More people were making more money than they ever had before. Thanks to the GI Bill, more students were enrolling in college than ever before. In Kentucky, a movement began to consolidate the schools, to merge smaller districts into larger ones, so the tiniest schools began to disappear. Many communities felt devastated and betrayed when their high school disappeared. And later, many observers thought that consolidation had, in fact, ripped the fabric of small towns across the state.

One thing, however, stayed exactly the same as it had been for years: Adolph Rupp and his University of Kentucky Wildcats continued to win basketball games. But for the first time in Rupp's career, serious trouble lay not far down the line.

AFTER BEARD AND GROZA ADMITTED TAKING MONEY FROM GAMBLERS TO SHAVE POINTS IN 1949, OTHER PLAYERS WERE IMPLICATED, TOO...DALE BARNSTABLE, WALT HIRSCH, JIM LINE. BUT BY 1951 ALL OF THEM HAD GRADUATED, AND RUPP WAS LOOKING FORWARD TO A SPECTACULAR SEASON WITH BILL SPIVEY, CLIFF HAGAN, FRANK RAMSEY, BOBBY WATSON, SHELBY LINVILLE, LOU TSIOROPOULOS, BILL EVANS AND A STRONG SUPPORTING CAST. THEY WERE RANKED NUMBER ONE FOR MOST OF THE SEASON, BUT LOST TO ST. JOHNS IN THE NCAA TOURNAMENT. WITH BILL SPIVEY, THEY COULD HAVE WON IT ALL. BUT SPIVEY WAS NOT ON THE TEAM. HE HAD WITHDRAWN TO CLEAR HIS NAME FROM THE FIX RUMORS THAT SWIRLED AROUND HIM. ALTHOUGH EXONERATED IN COURT, SPIVEY NEVER PLAYED ANOTHER GAME FOR UK.

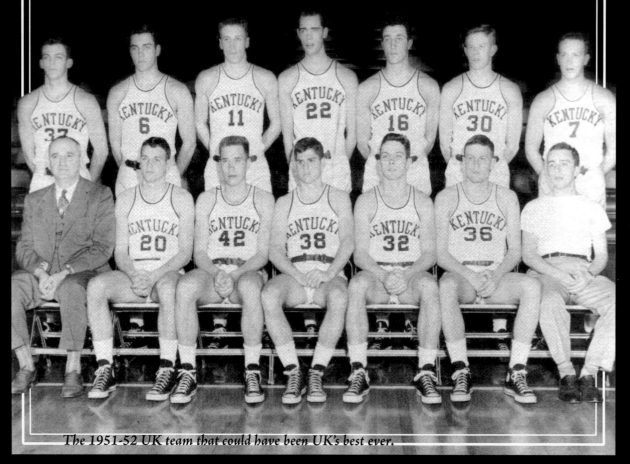

The 1951-52 UK team that could have been UK's best ever.

"To me, the biggest tragedy was Bill Spivey. He was the only guy who pleaded not guilty. He said he never took any money, and he was tried. He was the only one who went to trial. He was tried on a perjury charge, and the jury was hung, something like 9 to 3, in his favor. And he was never convicted of anything. He never admitted anything, and yet he was barred from the NBA for life."

~ BILLY REED

Mountain basketball reaches new heights

Mountain basketball announced its presence, at least as far back as 1928, when the famed Carr Creekers took Ashland to the wire in the Sweet Sixteen championship game before going on to national fame. That was just a beginning prior to consolidation. Eastern Kentucky probably produced more winning teams than any other region of the state. Some of the better-known coaches who established winning programs were John Bill Trivette at Pikeville, Goebel Ritter at Hazard, Pearl Combs at Whitesburg, and Russell Williamson at Inez. Nineteen-fifty-six might have been the best year ever for mountain basketball. Not only did Carr Creek, nearly 30 years after their first state championship appearance, go on to win it all, under Coach Morton Combs, but one player emerged who electrified the state. He was King Kelly Coleman, of the Wayland Wasps, and, neither before nor since, has there ever been another schoolboy player quite like the King.

ABOVE RIGHT: John Bill Trivette
ABOVE LEFT: Letcher Norton

King Kelly Coleman

"King Kelly Coleman came into the state tournament in 1956. Before the tournament, there were planes that flew over Lexington, dropping out leaflets that—'The King is Coming—the Greatest Thing to Come Out of Eastern Kentucky Since Coal.'" ～ Billy Reed

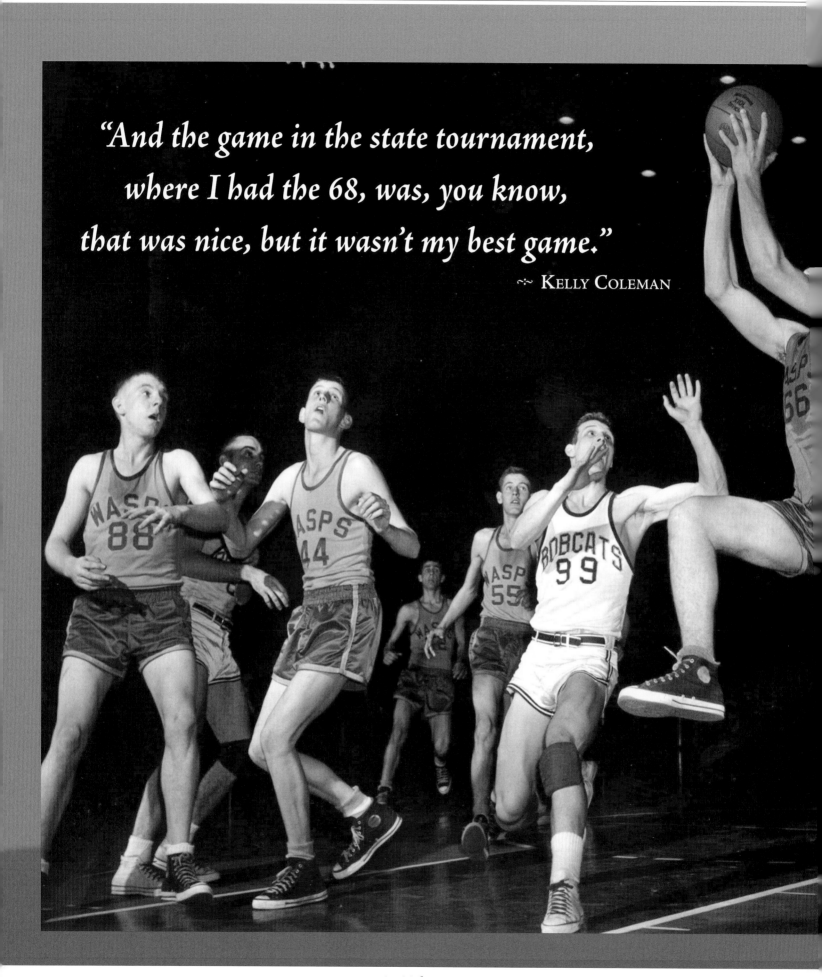

"And the game in the state tournament, where I had the 68, was, you know, that was nice, but it wasn't my best game."

~ KELLY COLEMAN

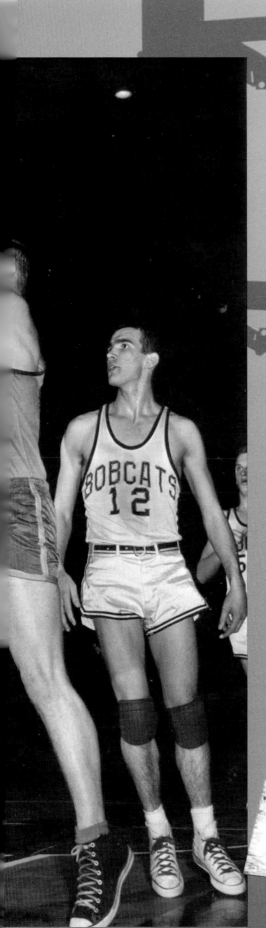

"*I remember well the first time I saw Kelly Coleman; he stood about six-three and had a belly on him and his shirttail hanging out; came across the center line in about three steps and knocked the bottom out.*"

~ MARCUS COMBS
CARR CREEK 1956

WELCOME
TO THE TOWN OF
WAYLAND
W
HOME OF THE
WASPS

"He got 60 to 65-some points. I don't know what it was, but I was at the game, and I thought I should go down and congratulate him. I said, 'Hey, King, can I see you a minute?' And he walked over. I said, 'I want to congratulate you.' I said, 'I'm Linville Puckett. I had the high school record here until you broke it.' And I said, 'I just want to say congratulations.' I stuck my hand out; his was just like a little dishrag. He just turned around and walked off. He didn't say nothing."

~ LINVILLE PUCKETT

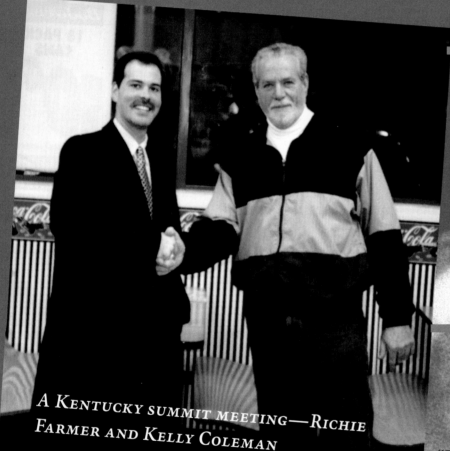

A KENTUCKY SUMMIT MEETING—RICHIE FARMER AND KELLY COLEMAN

"And the thing about being an athlete—it's not like being a lawyer or an architect or an engineer. They can make all these mistakes in their youth and when they're 40 years old they can do it over."

~ KELLY COLEMAN

"If I had gone to the University of Kentucky and played under Rupp—Coach Rupp—I probably would have taken a little different trail in life. You know, life is a road. You come to these crosses, and you've got to go one way or the other. And you have to make a choice and, most of the time, I think I made the wrong choice. When I should have gone right, I went left; and when I should have gone left, I went right."

~ KELLY COLEMAN

THE ARC OF KELLY
COLEMAN'S LIFE IS
STILL THE STUFF OF
KENTUCKY LEGEND—
PART HEROIC, PART
TRAGIC, A TOPIC OF
COFFEE-SHOP
CONVERSATION
NEARLY 50 YEARS
AFTER HIS PLAYING
DAYS.

Coach Peck Hickman rebuilds Louisville's team

"A lot of what he did, he patterned it after what he learned from Coach Diddle. It worked for Diddle, and Peck had some ideas — he had ideas of own and all that. But a lot of it was a carryover from his days at Western Kentucky."

Charlie Tyra

LEFT:
Louisville great John Turner tips in a shot in front of UK's Don Mills in 1959.

RIGHT:
Peck Hickman had played guard for Ed Diddle at Western Kentucky, and had been a highly successful coach at Valley High School in Louisville.

University of Louisville

In 1944, the University of Louisville hired Ed Diddle protégé Peck Hickman as the head coach of the men's basketball team, a position Hickman called "the worst job in America." But this would no longer be true by the time Hickman was finished. In his fourth year, U of L won the National Association of Intercollegiate Basketball Tournament, beating Indiana State, 82 to 70, and gaining, for the first time, national prominence. Then, in 1959, Louisville defeated defending National Champion Kentucky in the NCAA Tournament and earned a trip to the Final Four at Freedom Hall. In between, Louisville won the 1956 National Invitational Tournament, behind the play of star forward and ace rebounder Charlie Tyra, who, over a four-year career, averaged more than 18 points and 17 rebounds per game and who was twice a consensus All-American. With this team, Peck Hickman made sure everyone knew that Louisville was here to stay.

Basket Ball
DOUBLE HEADER

Men and Women

26 University of Louisville 11

vs.

15 University of Kentucky 8

Y. M. C. A.

February 27, 1915   Admission 50 Cents

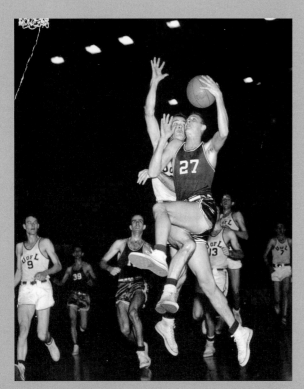

ABOVE: *Glen Combs, a star player on Hickman's third team in 1947, is about to block a shot.*

BELOW: *U of L vs. Duquesne, February 4, 1950. Kenny Reeves (13) and Bob Lochmueller (20) are among the Cardinals who won, 64-58.*

"When Peck Hickman, who played at Western Kentucky, took over the Louisville job in 1944, it was just the pits. I mean, his first few years there, I think he had to do everything from sweeping the floor at practice to washing the uniforms, and it was just really a nothing job."

~ BILLY REED

"Peck started with nothing. He was coaching Valley High School, out in Valley Station, in Jefferson County, last year of the war, and U of L hired him. And he had a little, bitty old bandbox gym, smaller than any high school gym I've ever seen."

~ EARL COX

U of L began playing its home games at the Armory in downtown Louisville in 1945.

RIGHT:

Cardinal great Don Goldstein was the star of the 1957-58 team.

"I think a lot of people think that Denny Crum might have invented Louisville basketball. But, believe me, it was Peck Hickman and John Dromo who really built that program to the point where Denny could come in and build on what they had done."

~ BILLY REED

The 1952-53 team: (top) Phil Rollins, Herb Hurrah, Chet Beam, Chuck Noble, Cliff York, Charles Harrison, Jerry Moreman; (middle) Coach Peck Hickman, Billy Powell, Vlad Gastevich, Bill Kidd, Al Russak, Frank Lentz, Bob Dunbar, Harry Hinton, coach John Dromo; (bottom) Dick Keffer, Bob Terrell, Corky Cox, Bill Sullivan, Bob Davis, Bill Newkirk; (on floor) managers John Reschar and Dave Archar.

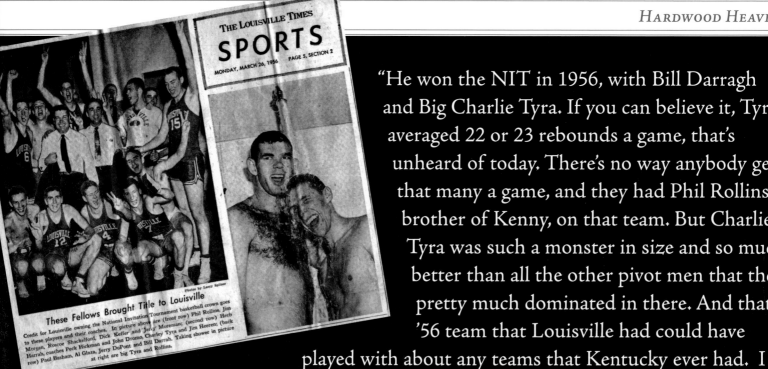

THE LOUISVILLE TIMES

SPORTS

MONDAY, MARCH 26, 1956   PAGE 5, SECTION 2

These Fellows Brought Title to Louisville

Credit for Louisville owning the National Invitation Tournament basketball crown goes to these players and their coaches. In picture above are (front row) Phil Rollins, Jim Morgan, Roscoe Shackelford, Dick Keffer and Jerry Moreman; (second row) Herb Harrah, coaches Peck Hickman and John Dromo, Charley Tyra and Jim Heeren; (back row) Paul Basham, Al Glaza, Jerry DuPont and Bill Darrah. Taking shower in picture at right are big Tyra and Rollins.

"He won the NIT in 1956, with Bill Darragh and Big Charlie Tyra. If you can believe it, Tyra averaged 22 or 23 rebounds a game, that's unheard of today. There's no way anybody gets that many a game, and they had Phil Rollins, brother of Kenny, on that team. But Charlie Tyra was such a monster in size and so much better than all the other pivot men that they pretty much dominated in there. And that '56 team that Louisville had could have played with about any teams that Kentucky ever had. I don't like to think that they could have beat the Fabulous Five, but I don't know that they couldn't. They were a heck of a team."

~ JOCK SUTHERLAND

"Well, I think any time you win a tournament like we did, and have the record, you start to draw a little bit of an attention to you. And we just had a group that the chemistry was right. I mean, it didn't matter if Charlie or any of the others got the most points; our main thought was we want to win that game."

~ BILL DARRAGH
U OF L 1957

"It was important, because it sort of legitimized the program. And it also made people who weren't aware that Peck Hickman was a pretty good coach and that we had a good program."

ABOVE: The 1956 NIT winners.

~ CHARLIE TYRA

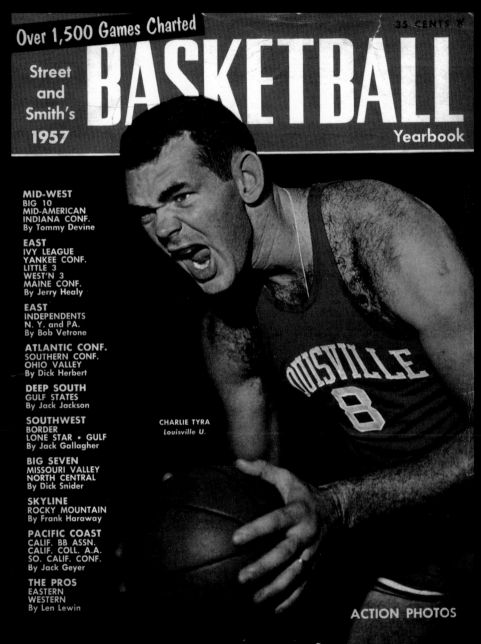

Over 1,500 Games Charted

35 CENTS

Street and Smith's 1957

BASKETBALL Yearbook

MID-WEST
BIG 10
MID-AMERICAN
INDIANA CONF.
By Tommy Devine

EAST
IVY LEAGUE
YANKEE CONF.
LITTLE 3
WEST'N 3
MAINE CONF.
By Jerry Healy

EAST
INDEPENDENTS
N. Y. and PA.
By Bob Vetrone

ATLANTIC CONF.
SOUTHERN CONF.
OHIO VALLEY
By Dick Herbert

DEEP SOUTH
GULF STATES
By Jack Jackson

SOUTHWEST
BORDER
LONE STAR • GULF
By Jack Gallagher

BIG SEVEN
MISSOURI VALLEY
NORTH CENTRAL
By Dick Snider

SKYLINE
ROCKY MOUNTAIN
By Frank Haraway

PACIFIC COAST
CALIF. BB ASSN.
CALIF. COLL. A.A.
SO. CALIF. CONF.
By Jack Geyer

THE PROS
EASTERN
WESTERN
By Len Lewin

CHARLIE TYRA
Louisville U.

ACTION PHOTOS

"I was in seventh grade when they won that NAIB Championship, and I read about it in the paper and saw the pictures of Jack Coleman and the Combs boys. They had Kenny Reeves, from Maysville, and they had another guy, Johnny Knopf, who went to Saint X, in Louisville. And the NAIB would be like a Division II or whatever — less than the NCAA or the NIT. But that was a big step. And really, Hickman did that in a fairly fast manner. I don't know what year he went to U of L. But from 1948 to 1956, to take that program from where it was to winning the NIT, which was the big deal, that's traveling pretty fast."

~ CHARLIE TYRA

HICKMAN GETS A VICTORY RIDE AFTER BEATING KENTUCKY 76-61 IN THE NCAA MIDWEST REGIONAL IN 1959. U OF L'S STARTERS WERE HAROLD ANDREWS AND ROGER TIEMAN AT GUARD, JOHN TURNER AND DON GOLDSTEIN AT FORWARD, AND FRED SAWYER, CENTER.

One of the most memorable games in Louisville basketball history was the 1961 NCAA regional game with Ohio State, which pitted UL's Fred Sawyer, Bud Olsen, John Turner, Howard Stacey and Jadie Frazier against Jerry Lucas, John Havlicek, Larry Siegfried and company. Despite leading by five with a few minutes to play, Louisville made mistakes down the stretch and Ohio State pulled out the win with a long Havlicek jumper and a missed free throw and shot by Turner at the buzzer. It was a sad end to a team Hickman thought could go all the way.

A disappointed John Turner (right) leaves the court with John Havlicek, whose jump shot with six seconds to go put the Buckeyes up by two. A free throw by Turner with one second to play pulled the Cards to within one, but the second missed, giving Ohio State the win, 56-55.

BELOW: *The 1964-65 team. (bottom) Tom Finnegan, Eddie Cramer, Dave Gilbert, Wade Houston; (top) John Reuther, Judd Rothman, Joe Liedtke. In 1962 Peck Hickman and John Dromo had recruited the university's first black players, Sam Smith, Wade Houston, and Eddie Whitehead.*

In 23 seasons, from 1944 to 1967, Peck Hickman's teams won 443 games, lost 183.

LEFT: John Reuther

BELOW: Fred Holden

"Coach Hickman was a very tough, demanding coach, and I learned a lot from him, particularly about defensive basketball, conditioning. We were fairly simple in offense; didn't do a lot of things on offense, but he was very, very demanding, in terms of conditioning and on the defensive end. And he very seldom smiled. We often thought of him as the meanest guy in the world."

~ WADE HOUSTON

Above: Wade Houston during his playing days. Later he became an assistant coach to Denny Crum, and a head coach at the University of Tennessee.

WESTLEY UNSELD HAD BEEN AN ALL-STATE
PLAYER AT SENECA, AND AT U OF L HE GREW A
BIT MORE TO 6-7 AND PUT ON WEIGHT AND
STRENGTH. SOON HE WAS VIRTUALLY
UNSTOPPABLE NEAR THE BASKET, OWNED THE
BACKBOARDS, THREW A TRADEMARK OUTLET
PASS ON THE BREAK, AND SET IMMOVABLE
PICKS. HIS TEAMMATE, BUTCH BEARD (14)
WAS MR. OUTSIDE TO UNSELD'S INSIDE, AND
TOGETHER THEY LED LOUISVILLE TO A #2
RANKING BEHIND LEW ALCINDOR AND UCLA
IN 1966.

A black basketball player, Irvine Shanks, of Richmond, quietly made his dramatic debut.

LEFT: *Irvine Shanks puts up a hook shot in a game in 1956. "In 1956 I was a pivot man..I'd be too short now, but back then it was OK. I never was a big scorer, but I loved rebounding, and that was my game."*

"It's a good thing to know that you kind of opened doors for people. You know, sometimes nowadays, I'll be sitting...you just think about things you've done in your life, and it's good to know that I was there. But when I was doing it, I never thought about it at all. It was just that I loved to play basketball."

❧ IRVINE SHANKS

Irvine Shanks and Berea

In 1904, the Kentucky Legislature passed the Day Law, which mandated racially segregated education for both public and private institutions. But in fact, the Day Law had one primary object: Berea College, which had been educating African-American students since 1866. Several years later, the Day Law was upheld by the U.S. Supreme Court, and Berea embarked upon a plan to create the Lincoln Institute, near Shelbyville, with the express purpose of educating black students, Day Law or no Day Law.

But in 1950, Berea began to once again admit African-American students, and in 1954 a black basketball player, Irvine Shanks, of Richmond, quietly made his dramatic debut.

"You don't think about it when it's actually happening. But now that I'm older, and I look back, it was a good opportunity for me to be in these positions. And that's the way I look at it when I think back."

~ IRVINE SHANKS

"The coach of the team, C.H. Wyatt, said, 'If any of our opponents don't like it, then we're playing him. We're not sitting him down. So we're going to have a game, whether you like it or not.' And that's what happened with Irvine Shanks."

~ TOM CHASE, AUTHOR

"Coach Wyatt, I think, should be remembered for a number of things. But the thing that really stands out in my mind, he was really the innovator. He was a pioneer in the integrating of college basketball."

~ ARNOLD THURMAN

Coach Wyatt of Berea

"At that time, there were restaurants that didn't allow any blacks in. And Coach Wyatt did a great job with this in that he would call ahead. He would make sure that we were going to be well received. And our philosophy was if they don't serve Irvine, we don't eat."

~ ARNOLD THURMAN

"The Greatest Show in Hoops."

WELCOME
TO THE
17th District Tournament

Bowling Green High School Gym

March 2, 3, 4, 5, 6 & 7, 1964

RC

ALVATON
BOWLING GREEN
BRISTOW
COLLEGE HIGH
FRANKLIN-SIMPSON
HIGH STREET
LINCOLN
NORTH WARREN
RICHARDSVILLE
ST. JOSEPH
WARREN COUNTY

PRICE 25¢

Sponsored by KEY CLUB B. G. H. S.

The Sweet Sixteen

The Sweet Sixteen remained one of the most popular institutions in all of Kentucky's sports throughout the '50s, '60s, and '70s. Traditional powers like Male, Lafayette, and Shelby County fielded great teams. Mountain teams like Inez continued to sneak away with the title, on occasion, and even Edmonson County, the ultimate Cinderella team, stole it all in '76. But this era was personified by players who would later become undisputed legends of the Sweet Sixteen. Butch Beard, Wes Unseld, Mike Casey and Darrell Griffith are just a few of the multi-talented stars who showcased their talents in what has come to be billed as "The Greatest Show in Hoops."

Inez, 1954

Inez, Kentucky state high school champs, 1954.

"Every place I go in Kentucky and have conversation with anybody my age or similar age, you know, they would find out you're from Inez. They bring that up, you know, 'Oh, that's the place that had great basketball teams at one time.'"

~ Carroll Justice, Inez 1955

"We were put in the same category as Cuba. You know, that '41 team was great; '37 was great. But I think, after that, Inez became known as the basketball capital, in eastern Kentucky, especially."

~ Dale Moore

Lexington Lafayette, 1950, 1953, 1957

Coach Jock Sutherland won a state title in 1979 with his star player, Dirk Minniefield.

Coach Ralph Carlisle won three state championships in the 1950s. His star in 1957, Billy Ray Lickert, went on to play for Rupp at Kentucky, and Carlisle himself was rumored to be the man who would follow Rupp as coach of the Wildcats. But it never happened.

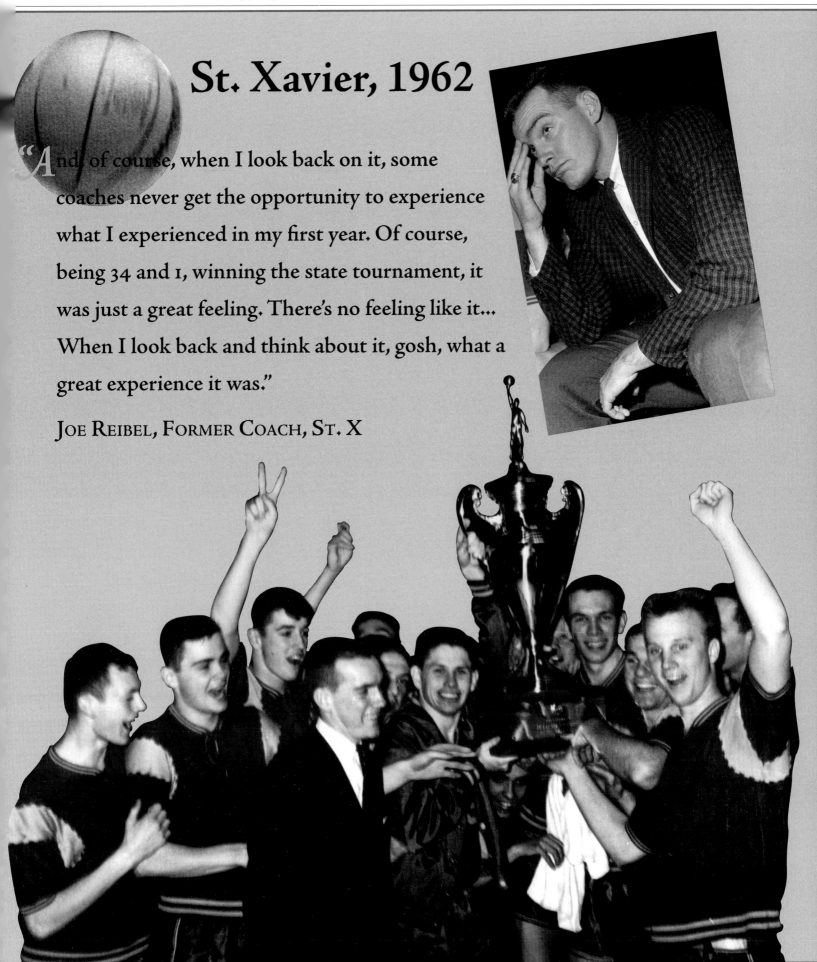

St. Xavier, 1962

"And of course, when I look back on it, some coaches never get the opportunity to experience what I experienced in my first year. Of course, being 34 and 1, winning the state tournament, it was just a great feeling. There's no feeling like it... When I look back and think about it, gosh, what a great experience it was."

JOE REIBEL, FORMER COACH, ST. X

Larry Conley, Gene Smith, Bob Hilton, Harold Sergent, and Steve Cram.

Ashland High School, 1961

"Best one I ever saw? It had to be one of the Louisville Central teams. But then I would have to say the Ashland Tomcats, 1961."   S.T. Roach

"Hal Sergent — we called him Peanut 'cause he was the smaller of the boys that we had on the varsity on the starting five — probably was one of the most outstanding young men you'll ever see. He had the fire; he had the confidence; he had everything that you needed."

~ BOB WRIGHT, FORMER HEAD COACH, ASHLAND HIGH SCHOOL

Star Larry Conley celebrates Ashland's win over S.T. Roach's Dunbar team.

Seneca High School, 1963, 1964

"It became the Mike Redd Show in 1963. Now, Mike was playing guard for us that year in 1963 and six-two. He was tough to handle because of his jumping ability, not that his size overpowered everyone. We had a set play for Mike in that we let him rub off the post and go set up in the low post area. He'd rub off Westley, and Westley Unseld was a formidable blocker. He could screen most anyone. In fact, that's what he did in the pros and so that would enable Mike not only slash to the basket off the dribble, but also to set up low and then take the outside shot as well. Westley Unseld was probably one of the finest young men that I've ever known, either in basketball, on the street, or anyplace."
—Bob Mulcahy, Former Head Coach, Seneca High School

WESTLEY UNSELD, 6-7, ALL-STATE FOR TWO YEARS AT SENECA.

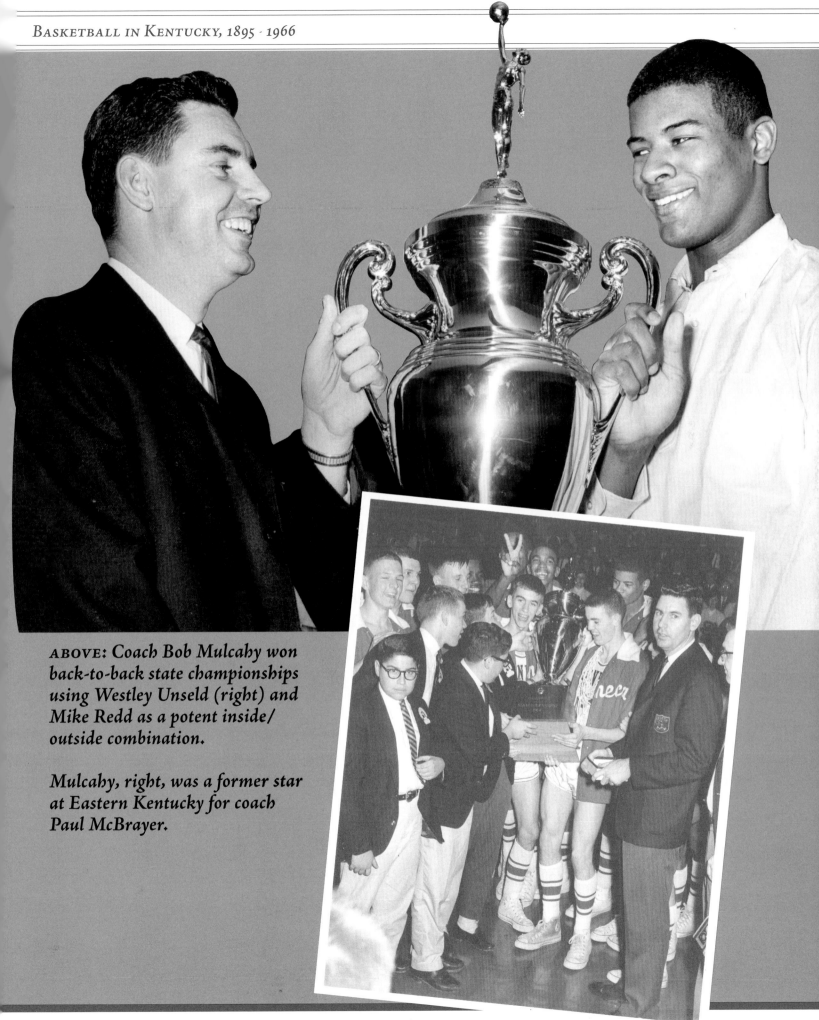

ABOVE: *Coach Bob Mulcahy won back-to-back state championships using Westley Unseld (right) and Mike Redd as a potent inside/ outside combination.*

Mulcahy, right, was a former star at Eastern Kentucky for coach Paul McBrayer.

Breckinridge County, 1965

BUTCH BEARD

'People will wonder, how did Butch Beard do his scoring? What great value did he really have to the team? Butch did it all. Butch would get the rebound. He would take it down the middle of the floor on the fast break. And he would either shoot or draw the defense on him. And then he would pass off to a teammate who was always wide open when Butch Beard made the pass off the fast break. He had that uncanny ability to get the ball to a man exactly at the right time, where he could score without any defensive contention. And Butch, basically, was the only player that was going to handle the ball, going down the middle of the floor. He either did it by receiving the return pass, or he did it by getting the rebound and coming off on the dribble and going to the middle of the floor himself, with his teammates filling in the lane on each side. The fast break and the press was our key, and Butch was the heart and soul of that particular offense and that style of play."

~~ Don Morris, former Head Coach,
Breckinridge County High School

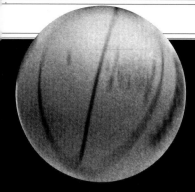

Shelby County, 1966

"There's players who can run up and down the floor quicker. There's players that can alley-oop dunk. But I don't think there's anybody that had as much desire, and just what it takes to win, as Mike Casey."

Bill Busey
SCHS, 1966

We were talking one time, and I said, 'Arnold, [Thurman] what do you want to accomplish?' He said, 'Well, one of my dreams has always been, on a Sunday morning, to be coming back from Louisville on a fire truck, holding the state championship trophy, riding through Shelbyville with my finger up in the air: 'We're number one!' And his dream came true."

~ BILL HARRELL, FORMER HEAD COACH, SHELBY COUNTY HIGH SCHOOL

VICTORIOUS SHELBY COUNTY BRINGS THE STATE CHAMPIONSHIP TROPHY TO SHELBYVILLE ON A FIRE TRUCK.

In some ways, the Ohio Valley Conference represents the very roots and essence of Kentucky basketball. For the OVC sprang from the Kentucky Intercollegiate Athletic Conference which had been formed in 1926, and which, at that time, represented nearly every institute of higher learning in Kentucky that put athletic teams on a field or in a gym. Following World War II, Louisville, Eastern, Western, and Morehead left the KIAC to form, along with several nearby out-of-state schools, the Ohio Valley Conference. Louisville soon left the conference, but each of the remaining schools made lasting contributions to Kentucky basketball. Ellis Johnson, star of Ashland High's 1928 team, coached Morehead's Golden Eagles from 1936 to 1953. Paul McBrayer, who played for Mrs. Kavanaugh, and was later an assistant coach at UK under Adolph Rupp for several seasons, coached Eastern Kentucky from 1946 to 1962. Stars like Bobby Washington later emerged for the Colonels.

Murray State, too, has had its share of successes and star players. Jumping Joe Fulks, who hailed from the Jackson Purchase area of far western Kentucky, starred as a Racer in the early '40s, went on to a successful NBA career and was eventually inducted into the Basketball Hall of Fame. Murray has continued to dominate the OVC , with players like NBA star Popeye Jones leading the way. But from 1949 to 1982, when the Hilltoppers left the OVC, Western Kentucky University was really first among equals. In that span, WKU won or shared the OVC title 20 times. And in 1971, seven years after Coach Ed Diddle's retirement, WKU played its way into an NCAA Final Four.

Ohio Valley Conference

LEFT: Joe Fulks is perhaps the most celebrated basketball player from Kentucky that you might not know. He was a star at every level—at Kuttawa High, where he led the school to its only state tournament; an All-American at Murray; a professional in the early days of the NBA, leading the league in scoring in 1947; and a member of the Basketball Hall of Fame.

"I know several people wanted me to use a red towel, and I said I wouldn't touch a red towel with a ten-foot pole. That was Coach Diddle; that wasn't me. He was very, very colorful. I was very gray. And so I didn't ever say I was replacing Coach Diddle, because nobody replaces a legend like Coach Diddle."

~ JOHN OLDHAM, FORMER COACH, WESTERN KENTUCKY UNIVERSITY

ABOVE: *Clem the Gem Haskins.*

RIGHT: *Western basketball royalty: Dee Gibson, Odie Spears, Don Ray, Oran McKinney, John Oldham.*

"Coach Diddle had recruited Dwight Smith and Clem Haskins, and they played freshman ball. Then I came in. So Coach Diddle really is credited with integrating, but Clem Haskins was the ideal black athlete, and Dwight Smith was the ideal. So let's say that Coach Diddle really gave me a nucleus of two great black athletes to start with."

~ JOHN OLDHAM

RIGHT AND BELOW: *Clem Haskins was an All-American forward for the Hilltoppers.*

BELOW: *Dwight Smith, Haskins' running mate at guard.*

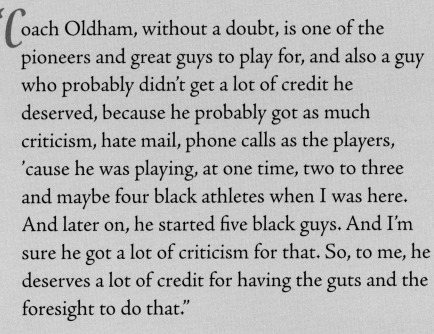

"Coach Oldham, without a doubt, is one of the pioneers and great guys to play for, and also a guy who probably didn't get a lot of credit he deserved, because he probably got as much criticism, hate mail, phone calls as the players, 'cause he was playing, at one time, two to three and maybe four black athletes when I was here. And later on, he started five black guys. And I'm sure he got a lot of criticism for that. So, to me, he deserves a lot of credit for having the guts and the foresight to do that."

~ CLEM HASKINS

Western star Dwight Smith signs with the Lakers, but becomes a victim of tragedy, drowning in an auto accident shortly after his last college game.

"Dwight Smith was one of the best players I ever played with or played against in my whole life. And he was a six-five guy who could guard a guy five-five or guard a guy six-ten; a tremendous defensive player."

~ CLEM HASKINS

"He [Dwight Smith] was the most athletic person on our team. He was the best basketball player on our team. He could shoot the ball. He was a six-five point guard. He could play defense. He was tremendously quick. He could jump out of the gym. Dwight would have been a starter in the NBA for years with the Los Angeles Lakers, because he'd just come back from a trip out there, to be evaluated, and they were going to sign him the following week of his death. And it was just tragic that he died in a car wreck before he could do that."

~ WAYNE CHAPMAN

ABOVE: *Brothers Greg (left) and Dwight Smith.*
LEFT: *Wayne Chapman*

Paul McBrayer, shown at right with one of his early Eastern teams, was an All-American at Kentucky in 1930 in then-coach John Mauer's last year.

Garfield Smith dominated around the basket.

Below, Eastern's great Bobby Washington.

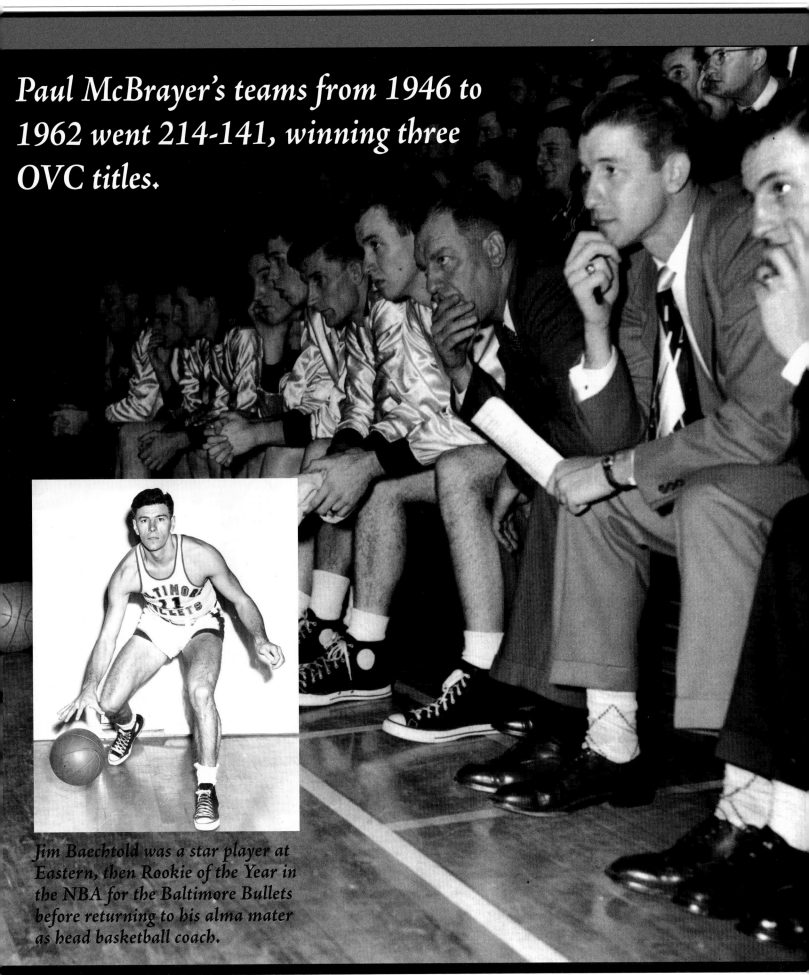

Paul McBrayer's teams from 1946 to 1962 went 214-141, winning three OVC titles.

Jim Baechtold was a star player at Eastern, then Rookie of the Year in the NBA for the Baltimore Bullets before returning to his alma mater as head basketball coach.

MOREHEAD

At Morehead, Ellis Johnson of '28 Ashland and UK fame, coached for 15 years, going 176-158 and adding to the colorful legacy of OVC coaches.

LEFT: One of Morehead's great players was Sonny Allen (third from left).

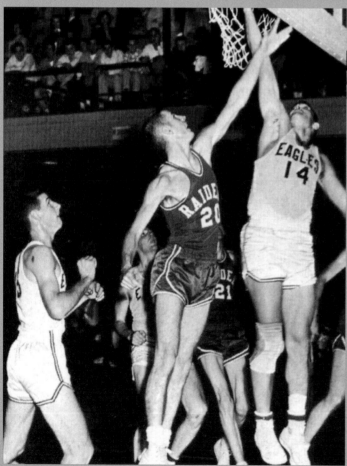

ABOVE: Coach Bobby Laughlin coached Morehead to four OVC titles in twelve years.

LEFT: Steve Hamilton was a multi-sport star at Morehead, and continued his versatility in the pros, playing both basketball and baseball professionally.

Dan Swartz (14) was a dominating player.

MURRAY STATE

Former Murray State Head Coach Cal Luther coached the Racers from 1958 to 1974, compiling a 241-154 record, with three Ohio Valley Conference titles.

CAL LUTHER

Joe Fulks (above and at right, center of top row) is still the standard by which Murray State's players are measured. A shooter, Fulks led the team in points scored, and in his NBA career held the single game scoring record (63) for eleven years.

Kentucky Wesleyan wins three NCAA Division II titles in four years, from 1966 to 1969.

UCLA has won 11 NCAA titles, more than any other school. What school is in second place, behind UCLA? And here's a clue: It's not the University of Kentucky Wildcats, with seven. No, Kentucky Wesleyan has won eight NCAA Division II titles, including three out of four in the years 1966 through 1969, as well as the 1987 and 1990 teams, coached by Wayne Chapman. More recently, the Ray Harper-coached Panthers appeared in four straight championship games, from 1998 to 2001, winning twice and putting together a string of four straight 30-win seasons. Panther fans are proud to note that, for the most successful basketball program in Kentucky, you bypass Lexington and Louisville and go straight to Owensboro.

1996 NCAA Division II National Champions - Don Bradley, George Tinsley, Sam Smith, Roger Cordell, Dallas Thornton, Jesse Flynn, Danny Barker, Tom Hobgood, John Chapman, Joel Bolden, Ernie Simpson, Steve Deskins, Jim Arington, Tom Vittitow (Manager), Dick Kirtley (Manager), Dick Romer (Manager), Bob Daniels (Assistant Coach), and Guy Strong (Head Coach).

RIGHT: *The first of eight NCAA titles came in 1966.*

FACING PAGE: *Kelly Coleman wound up playing for Kentucky Wesleyan after his high school career, and became an All-American.*

"Kentucky Wesleyan College's first national championship, in 1966, Guy Strong was the head coach. And there had been a couple of lean years in there just before he came. He built a program. He did a good job of recruiting, bringing in some local guys, mostly state players. But we ended up with a very good team. If you want to go back and look at the start of the national championships, he won the first one, and that helped to start that tradition, to help Kentucky Wesleyan College be where it is today."

~ BOB DANIELS, COACH
KENTUCKY WESLEYAN, 1968-1972

Race issues play a role in the 1966 NCAA championship.

RIGHT: *The Runts—Pat Riley, Larry Conley, Thad Jaracz, Tommy Kron, Louie Dampier.*

BELOW: *Louie Dampier was one of the deadliest outside shots in Kentucky basketball history.*

"Rupp began the 1965 season with an unlikely collection of smallish players who would become, perhaps, the most loved team in the history of UK basketball. The group, known as 'Rupp's Runts', won 27 of 28 games before falling to Texas Western in the 1966 NCAA finals."

~ CAWOOD LEDFORD

"Rupp's Runts"

*I*n the 1966 Final Four, the assembled teams were Utah, Duke, The University of Kentucky, and Texas Western. Texas Western started an all-black squad, while both Duke and Kentucky, positioned in the opposite bracket, were all-white teams.

No matter how the Final Four played out, race was going to be part of the drama.

TOP LEFT: *Pat Riley was often at a height disadvantage, but was a strong, determined, and gifted athlete.*

ABOVE: *Cawood Ledford, Voice of the Wildcats.*

LEFT: *The Cats hung a loss on mighty Michigan, with All-American Cazzie Russell.*

RIGHT: *Adolph Rupp and Assistant Coach (soon to be Head Coach) Joe B. Hall.*

Underdog Texas Western defeats Kentucky to take the 1966 NCAA Championship.

Kentucky beat Duke, and Texas Western beat the Utes to set up the finals. Texas Western was a huge underdog to the talent and experience of the Cats. But the quicker, more aggressive Texas Western team won.

And some observers across the nation saw in the game something like a victory for civil rights. But there is one point that cannot be argued: the loss to Texas Western was a huge disappointment to Coach Adolph Rupp.

The 1965-66 University of Kentucky team.

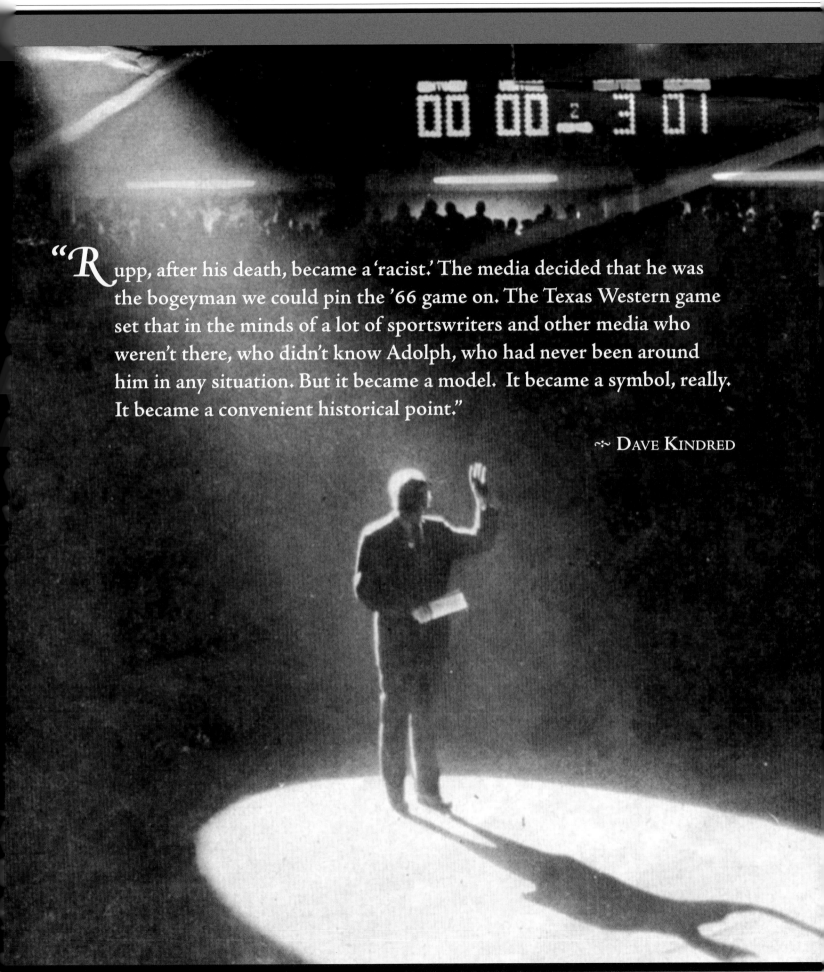

"Rupp, after his death, became a 'racist.' The media decided that he was the bogeyman we could pin the '66 game on. The Texas Western game set that in the minds of a lot of sportswriters and other media who weren't there, who didn't know Adolph, who had never been around him in any situation. But it became a model. It became a symbol, really. It became a convenient historical point."

~ DAVE KINDRED

BELOW: *Adolph Rupp signs his first black player, Tom Payne, in 1969. Payne would play only the 1970-71 season before jumping to the NBA's Atlanta Hawks.*

Kentucky State's Travis Grant (33) and Elmore Smith (25).

Louisville's Darrell Griffith

"The one thing I am sure, in my heart and mind, is that he was not a racist. Coach Rupp looked at people as people; but he was a pragmatist. He was very realistic. And I know in my heart it wouldn't have mattered to him if they were black or purple; if guys could play and act right and so on, they would have been welcome on his basketball team."

~ C.M. NEWTON

Kentucky's Jamal Mashburn

The Modern Era

Whether Kentucky's loss to Texas Western was an historical marker or not, no one could argue that the game of basketball in the late 1960s and '70s was changing. African-American players became the rule, not the exception, on most college teams, and the overall size, speed, and caliber of players at every level increased. Coaching techniques and systems became more complex, and strength training became a part of every major program. The Modern Era had begun, and the old game of crip shots, underhand foul shots and the two-hand set was gone forever.

Kentucky's Kenny Walker

Western Kentucky's Jim McDaniels

Louisville's Rodney McCray

"When I see a basketball game, I see different versions of life stories being played out. My idea of sports is that you go to see ordinary people doing extraordinary things, and extraordinary people doing unimaginable things.

"The Greeks said that anything beautiful in motion enhances life; it enlarges life; and there's no game that's better at watching the poetry, bodies in motion, the geometric shapes changing constantly, than basketball."

—*Dave Kindred*